SYRIA
THROUGH
JIHADIST EYES:
A PERFECT ENEMY

HERBERT AND JANE DWIGHT WORKING GROUP
ON ISLAMISM AND THE INTERNATIONAL ORDER

*Many of the writings associated with this
Working Group will be published by the
Hoover Institution. Materials published to date,
or in production, are listed below.*

ESSAYS

Saudi Arabia and the New Strategic Landscape
Joshua Teitelbaum

Islamism and the Future of the Christians of the Middle East
Habib C. Malik

Syria through Jihadist Eyes: A Perfect Enemy
Nibras Kazimi

The Ideological Struggle for Pakistan
Ziad Haider

BOOKS

Freedom or Terror: Europe Faces Jihad
Russell A. Berman

HERBERT & JANE DWIGHT WORKING GROUP ON ISLAMISM AND THE INTERNATIONAL ORDER

Syria
through
Jihadist Eyes:
A Perfect Enemy

Nibras Kazimi

HOOVER INSTITUTION PRESS
Stanford University   Stanford, California

Hoover Institution Press Publication No. 586
Hoover Institution at Leland Stanford Junior University, Stanford, California, 94305–6010

First printing 2010
16 15 14 13 12 11 10   9 8 7 6 5 4 3 2 1

Manufactured in the United States of America

The paper used in this publication meets the minimum Requirements of the American National Standard for Information Sciences— Permanence of Paper for Printed Library Materials, ANSI/NISO Z39.48–1992. ⊗

Cataloging-in-Publication Data is available from the Library of Congress.
ISBN 978-0-8179-1075-4 (pbk.)
ISBN 978-0-8179-1076-1 (e-book)

The Hoover Institution gratefully acknowledges
the following individuals and foundations
for their significant support of the

HERBERT AND JANE DWIGHT WORKING GROUP
ON ISLAMISM AND THE INTERNATIONAL ORDER

Herbert and Jane Dwight
Stephen Bechtel Foundation
Lynde and Harry Bradley Foundation
Mr. and Mrs. Clayton W. Frye Jr.
Lakeside Foundation

Contents

Foreword

For decades, the themes of the Hoover Institution have revolved around the broad concerns of political and economic and individual freedom. The cold war that engaged and challenged our nation during the twentieth century guided a good deal of Hoover's work, including its archival accumulation and research studies. The steady output of work on the communist world offers durable testimonies to that time, and struggle. But there is no repose from history's exertions, and no sooner had communism left the stage of history than a huge challenge arose in the broad lands of the Islamic world. A brief respite, and a meandering road, led from the fall of the Berlin Wall on 11/9 in 1989 to 9/11. Hoover's newly launched project, the Herbert and Jane Dwight Working

Group on Islamism and the International Order, is our contribution to a deeper understanding of the struggle in the Islamic world between order and its nemesis, between Muslims keen to protect the rule of reason and the gains of modernity, and those determined to deny the Islamic world its place in the modern international order of states. The United States is deeply engaged, and dangerously exposed, in the Islamic world, and we see our working group as part and parcel of the ongoing confrontation with the radical Islamists who have declared war on the states in their midst, on American power and interests, and on the very order of the international state system.

The Islamists are doubtless a minority in the world of Islam. But they are a determined breed. Their world is the Islamic emirate, led by self-styled "emirs and mujahedeen in the path of God" and legitimized by the pursuit of the caliphate that collapsed with the end of the Ottoman Empire in 1924. These masters of terror and their foot soldiers have made it increasingly difficult to integrate the world of Islam into modernity. In the best of worlds, the entry of Muslims into modern culture and economics would have presented difficulties of no small consequence: the strictures on women, the legacy of humiliation and self-pity, the outdated educational systems, and an explosive demography that is forever at war with social and economic gains. But the borders these warriors of the faith have erected between Islam and "the other" are particularly forbidding. The lands of Islam were the lands of a crossroads civilization, trading routes and mixed populations. The Islamists have waged war, and a brutally effective one it has to be conceded, against that civilizational inheritance. The leap into the modern world economy as attained by China and India in recent years will be virtually impossible in a culture that feeds off belligerent self-pity, and endlessly calls for wars of faith.

The war of ideas with radical Islamism is inescapably central to this Hoover endeavor. The strategic context of this clash, the landscape of that Greater Middle East, is the other pillar. We face three layers of danger in the heartland of the Islamic world: states that have succumbed to the sway of terrorists in which state authority no longer exists (Afghanistan, Somalia, and Yemen), dictatorial regimes that suppress their people at home and pursue deadly weapons of mass destruction and adventurism abroad (Iraq under Saddam Hussein, the Iranian theocracy), and "enabler" regimes, such as the ones in Egypt and Saudi Arabia, which export their own problems with radical Islamism to other parts of the Islamic world and beyond. In this context, the task of reversing Islamist radicalism and of reforming and strengthening the state across the entire Muslim world—the Middle East, Africa, as well as South, Southeast, and Central Asia—is the greatest strategic challenge of the twenty-first century. The essential starting point is detailed knowledge of our enemy.

Thus, the working group will draw on the intellectual resources of Hoover and Stanford and on an array of scholars and practitioners from elsewhere in the United States from the Middle East and the broader world of Islam. The scholarship on contemporary Islam can now be read with discernment. A good deal of it, produced in the immediate aftermath of 9/11, was not particularly deep and did not stand the test of time and events. We, however, are in the favorable position of a "second generation" assessment of that Islamic material. Our scholars and experts can report, in a detailed, authoritative way, on Islam within the Arabian Peninsula, on trends within Egyptian Islam, on the struggle between the Kemalist secular tradition in Turkey, and on the new Islamists, particularly the fight for the loyalty of European Islam between these who accept the canon, and the discipline, of modernism and those who don't.

Arabs and Muslims need not be believers in American exceptionalism, but our hope is to engage them in this contest of ideas. We will not necessarily aim at producing primary scholarship, but such scholarship may materialize in that our participants are researchers who know their subjects intimately. We see our critical output as essays accessible to a broader audience, primers about matters that require explication, op-eds, writings that will become part of the public debate, and short, engaging books that can illuminate the choices and the struggles in modern Islam.

We see this endeavor as a faithful reflection of the values that animate a decent, moderate society. We know the travails of modern Islam, and this working group will be unsparing in depicting them. But we also know that the battle for modern Islam is not yet lost, that there are brave men and women fighting to retrieve their faith from the extremists. Some of our participants will themselves be intellectuals and public figures who have stood up to the pressure. The working group will be unapologetic about America's role in the Muslim world. A power that laid to waste religious tyranny in Afghanistan and despotism in Iraq, that came to the rescue of the Muslims in the Balkans when they appeared all but doomed, has given much to those burdened populations. We haven't always understood Islam and Muslims—hence this inquiry. But it is a given of the working group that the pursuit of modernity and human welfare, and of the rule of law and reason, in Islamic lands is the common ground between America and contemporary Islam.

SYRIA SITS ASTRIDE the divide between Iran and its Arab rivals. The regime in Damascus goes along with the theocrats in Iran, facilitating their access to Lebanon and to the Palestinian territories, but hints that it is open to accommodation with Israel and a strategic bargain with the United States. No sooner did he come into office than President Barack Obama signaled he was ready to cut a deal with the Syrian rulers. Gone was the Bush diplomacy that had ended a thirty-year Syrian occupation of Lebanon and an overall American policy that put Syria beyond the pale.

Nibras Kazimi, a young, incisive writer on Arab affairs, challenges Obama's facile reading of Syria and its presumed readiness for peace and normalcy. With field notes accumulated in a Syrian environment not particularly hospitable to research and inquiry, Kazimi provides a unique view of the Syrian regime and its base at home. His unsparing portrait of the tension between a minority regime dominated by Alawite soldiers and its majority Sunni population reminds us of the hazards of betting on autocracies that lack a decent social contract between ruler and ruled. A poignant irony is at the heart of this historically luminous study: the Syrians aid and abet the jihad in Iraq, although they themselves are the dreaded enemies of the same (Sunni) jihadists. There are works of apology for the Syrian regime, and other works that fly at a very high altitude from Syrian realities. Kazimi fills a void in our understanding of the intelligence barons and soldiers—and the dominant family—who run that country.

Fouad Ajami,
Senior Fellow, Hoover Institution
Co-chairman, Herbert and Jane Dwight Working Group on Islamism and the International Order

Syria through Jihadist Eyes: A Perfect Enemy

Nibras Kazimi

INTRODUCTION

As Islamic extremists look for a new place to challenge the West in their pursuit of global jihad, their eyes are likely to turn to Syria. President Obama has indicated he wants to normalize relations with this small country and its apparently stable, although dictatorial, government. But Syria is in many ways ripe for change, and violent change at that. Location is part of the equation. Syria borders on five of the hottest hot spots in the Middle East: Iraq, Turkey, Lebanon, Israel, and Jordan. But more important are that ancient nation's place in history and its religious make-up. Historically, Syria is a place where the two leading branches of Islam, the Sunnis and the Shi'as, have often clashed. Religiously, Syria's population is mostly Sunni; however, members of a small sect that identifies itself with the minority Shi'as have been in power for forty years. These are the Nusayri-'Alawites, whose obscure history, secretive religious practices, and role as the target of Sunni fatwas over many centuries combine with their powerful position in modern Syria to provide a potential flashpoint for jihadists from around the world.

> *"Imagine if the Native Americans managed to regroup and to reoccupy America . . . and then you will know what Syrian President Hafez al-Asad managed to do with the 'Alawites."*[1]

This quotation highlights the feeling among many Syrians that the capture of power in their country by the Nusayri-'Alawites, a historically rural minority, is a fluke of history. The orthodox Sunnis were never supposed to be ruled over by Shi'a religious "dissenters" (as Sunnis depict the Shi'a), much less by a marginal and browbeaten heterodox Shi'a group such as the Nusayri-'Alawites, which was historically

2

considered to be outside of the mainstream by Sunnis and Shi'as alike. As one Sunni Islamist tract put it, it is against "the logic of things . . . The [Nusayri-'Alawite] minority has forgotten itself and is ignoring the facts of history."[2]

The Nusayri-'Alawites, still the ruling class in Syria after nearly four decades, comprise no more than 15 percent of the population, but they lord it over a Sunni Arab majority of at least 55 percent. A Sunni loyalist elite, which enjoys what one scholar called "derivative power" devolved onto it by the Nusayri-'Alawites, is a critical component of the power structure and colludes in this abnormal power balance, with the aim of obscuring the blatant sectarianism of the regime. However, for other Sunnis, this façade of shared power is not enough to allay their wrath. It is the aim of this paper to consider how the "jihadists," the global fraternity of militant Islamists, understand this historical aberration and how they seek to address it. The conclusion is that they will strive to correct it, violently.

In a speech produced four months before his death, Abu Musa'ab al-Zarqawi—the leader of the jihad in Iraq since 2003 who introduced revolutionary changes in jihadist tactics and ideology up to his death by a U.S. airstrike in June 2006—married traditional Wahhabi-inspired anti-Shi'ism to the strategic goals of worldwide jihad. Al-Zarqawi concluded that one of the goals of jihad should be the wholesale annihilation of Shi'as in theaters of war in which the jihadists are engaged, as a precursor to fighting the West and Israel. Al-Zarqawi argued that the Shi'as constituted the internal enemy within Islam, tantamount to a "fifth column," forever enabling the faith's enemies from without. Few have pondered the grave implications of al-Zarqawi's strategic vision for long-term stability in Syria, a country where a hated minority heterodox Shi'a sect rules, and that may become a natural outlet for the hateful, pent-up sectarian energies released by al-Zarqawi.

Al-Zarqawi's world view is too radical even for traditional Wahhabism, which was loathe to propose wholesale massacre of mainstream Shi'a laypersons, reserving punishment of death to the Shi'a elite only. This was a reluctance that al-Zarqawi felt he needed to address when explaining his "final solution." However, the

Nusayri-'Alawites fall under a different category outside of mainstream Shi'ism; the ideological founts from which the Wahhabis draw inspiration, such as fourteenth-century scholar Ibn Taymiyya, had proposed mass annihilation for the Nusayri-'Alawites during his time. Al-Zarqawi had to invent doctrinal excuses for exterminating Iraqi Shi'as to assuage Sunni reservations and scruples. With the Nusayri-'Alawites of Syria, however, there are no holds barred.

For jihadist purposes, the Nusayri-'Alawites constitute a "perfect enemy" in ideological and strategic aspects,[3] or at least one that is most convenient. Two factors are of particular importance: first, earlier generations of jihadists, spawned by the extremist wing of the Syrian Muslim Brethren, had tried to confront the Syrian regime; and second, Syria has great symbolic and strategic value for Sunni Islam. Therefore, it is conceivable that the Zarqawists who have been active in Iraq and elsewhere may direct their talents and resources toward fomenting an anti-Nusayri-'Alawite jihad in Syria.

This paper will not dwell on Nusayri-'Alawite religious tenets, and the history of the sect will be examined only as it relates to how Sunnis perceive them to be a threat to their very existence, past and present.[4] Nor shall it delve into the formation of a separate state for the Nusayri-'Alawites during the French mandate era (1923–1943), the history of the Ba'ath Party's takeover in the 1960s, the biography of President Hafez al-Asad (who assumed undisputed power in 1970), or the events of the Sunni Islamist revolt spanning the late 1970s and early 1980s. All have been amply covered by other works that are referred to, where appropriate, in the endnotes.

The framework of this paper is speculative and conceptual: a jihadist insurgency in Syria has yet to declare itself with a systematic campaign of violence against the regime and the Nusayri-'Alawite populace. But this paper does seek to capture a moment in time during which the jihadists deliberate the question, "Where to next, after the Iraq and Afghanistan fronts?" Some jihadist strategists perceive the Iraqi and Afghan theaters to have become wars of attrition with the West, rather than conduits to outright victory. The paper before you acknowledges the jihadist opponent as a strategic creature, and it aims to figure out his next move, and what tactical, propagandist, and strategic ingredients are required, in jihadist eyes, for success. It strives to get inside jihadist thinking on whether these ingredients are available in Syria.

This paper first examines the textual foundations from which the jihadists may draw inspiration to cast the Nusayri-'Alawites as beyond the pale of acceptable and redeemable religious differences. Next is a description of how Sunnis have traditionally viewed the Nusayri-'Alawites as a threat (in medieval and modern times) and as nothing more than a nuisance (in between). A look at what jihadist ideologues and strategists have had to say on the topic is followed by what is essentially a "travelogue" account of five extended field trips to Syria conducted by the author between March 2006 and July 2007. The author collected conversations concerning the rising tenor of sectarianism and how minority sects believe they are unfairly viewed by Sunnis, and how Sunnis approach this perceived threat. In conclusion, I assess how sectarianism and the global jihadist interest in taking the battle to Syria could derail policy overtures from Washington which are aimed at normalizing relations with the Asad regime after a period of outright hostility between the United States and Syria.

A NOTE ON THE TERMS "NUSAYRI-'ALAWITE" AND "BILAD AL-SHAM"

"Nusayri" is perceived to be a derogatory name for Nusayri-'Alawites. However, it is the name by which they have been known for most of their existence. At certain times in their history, they have adopted it, and the members of their community in southern Turkey still call themselves by it. "Alawite" is an early twentieth-century formulation, meant to put some distance between the sect and its despised status in the past. However, most jihadist tracts refer to them only as "Nusayri" and it has become an academic standard to combine the two terms. "Bilad al-sham," a geographic term historically used to describe the region around Damascus but which has come to be used for the area that Western sources describe as "the Levant," shall be translated as "Greater Syria."

THE LEGACY OF TEXTUAL INCITEMENTS TO JIHAD

Ibn Taymiyya (1263–1328), by far the most important source of inspiration for today's jihadists, lived in very difficult times for orthodox Islam. A scion of a family displaced from northern Syria to Damascus by the Mongol hordes, he observed that Islam as he understood it and believed in it had been under attack and undermined for several centuries. By the time he picked up a pen the external threat had been checked and it was imperative upon a resurgent orthodoxy to confront the internal heresies that had sprung up during the past chaos. Chief among his heretical targets were the Nusayri-'Alawites. He believed they represented a threat, one dangerous enough to put an end to Sunnism, and one which must be stamped out. It is no accident that Sunni revivalists in the twentieth century turned to his words for succor and guidance when confronted by circumstances similar to those witnessed by Ibn Taymiyya. Similarly in modern times, when Nusayri-'Alawites were recast as a threat to Sunnism, Ibn Taymiyya was trotted out to cast the sectarians as outside the faith, and to make the point that drastic actions, amounting to annihilation, were warranted. No other Muslim thinker commands the amount of reverence that modern jihadists hold for Ibn Taymiyya. The fact that Ibn Taymiyya armed the jihadists with a blueprint as to how to handle a Nusayri-'Alawite threat releases them from the task of coming up with a doctrinally sound argument for why drastic measures are now warranted. His word is akin to scripture, and he has shown them the way forward.

Three fatwas are attributed to Ibn Taymiyya regarding the Nusayri-'Alawites. In each, he sought to establish a relevant Islamic precedent. No chronological order can be discerned, but it is likely that the first fatwa[5] dealt with such questions as the sect's deification of the Prophet Muhammad's son-in-law, Ali ibn Abi

Taleb, whether Muslims can intermarry with members of the sect or allow them to be buried in Muslim cemeteries, and whether they could be trusted with the protection of Islamic lands against non-Muslims. The questioner also asks whether their blood and wealth are sanctioned for the taking and whether a Nusayri-ʿAlawite fighting against the enemy, in that case the Crusaders,[6] is considered a *murabit*, or holy warrior holding territory at the edges of the land of Islam. It is likely that this fatwa was commissioned in order to mobilize support for the Mameluke raids into Kisrawan, in Lebanon, and in the Dhinniyah mountains east of Tripoli, areas that were seemingly settled by heterodox sects, chief among them the Nusayri-ʿAlawites, in 1305 AD.[7]

Irrespective of the errors that Ibn Taymiyya made in identifying the tenets of Nusayri-ʿAlawism, or in confusing them with other sects, his fatwa cast the Nusayri-ʿAlawites among the sects whose danger to Islam is greater than that of the Mongols or the Crusaders. He characterized them as seeking to identify themselves as mainstream Shiʾas, whereas in reality "they do not believe in Allah, or [Muhammad], or the [Koran]" and disregard all the obligations of being a Muslim with the excuse that esoteric knowledge exempts them from praying, fasting, or making the pilgrimage to Mecca. As such, precedent places them among the *kuffar* (unbelievers) and the heretics, and those who reject Islam, which they take to extents "further than that of the Jews and Christians and the Brahmins of India who worship deities." Ibn Taymiyya adds a political dimension by stating that groups such as the Nusayri-'Alawites always ally themselves with the enemies of the Muslims, and that they enabled the Crusaders' conquest of Jerusalem. "Their religion externally is [Shi'ism] but internally it is pure unbelief," and Muslim precedent has ruled that they are not to be coupled with or married,[8] and the meat they slaughter is not *halal*. They may not be buried in Muslim cemeteries, and they may not be employed to defend Muslim lands, for that would be "like entrusting the wolf to shepherd the lambs." Their blood and wealth are sanctioned for the taking, and even if they show repentance and follow Islam, their progeny should not be allowed to inherit their wealth, which should revert to the Islamic treasury. Furthermore, their repentance could be a deception, and to make sure that orthodoxy takes hold among them they should be dispersed and monitored, and never employed in the warrior class; furthermore, religious scholars should live among them to teach them Islam.

The second fatwa concerned both the Druze and the Nusayri-'Alawites, and Ibn Taymiyya found precedent in calling them apostates from Islam, non-Muslim, and neither Jewish nor Christian. It is shorter and more concise, culminating in him saying that "the unbelief of [the Nusayri-'Alawites and the Druze] is not questioned by the Muslims, in fact whoever questions their unbelief is himself an unbeliever, for they are not in the category of [Christians and Jews] or polytheists, but rather deceptive unbelievers, it is forbidden to eat their food, their women are to be [taken into concubinage], their money seized, they are heretic apostates whose repentance is not accepted, and they must be killed wherever found, and to be cursed as described . . . their scholars and [notables] must be killed so that they would not lead others astray . . . it is forbidden to sleep with them in their houses, or to walk with them and accompany them, and to attend their funerals if announced, and it is forbidden for rulers to [neglect] what Allah ordered as punishments for them [for the sake of expediency]."[9]

The third and final fatwa seemed to have been a response to a messianic insurrection among Nusayri-'Alawites in 1317.[10] It is no less radical than its predecessors, and even addressed whether young children of the Nusayri-'Alawites were to be taken as slaves or freed. Ibn Taymiyya asserts that the Nusayri-'Alawites should be fought even without the prompting or excuse of a false messiah appearing among them or of them being in a state of revolt.[11]

Beyond Ibn Taymiyya, the Ottomans, self-styled defenders of Sunni internationalism, commissioned fatwas relating to their struggle against the Shi'a Safavids (rulers of Persia from 1502–1722) that were applicable against the

Nusayri-'Alawites, with whom they began to come into contact as they expanded into Greater Syria in the sixteenth century. But it wasn't until the nineteenth century that another influential fatwa was rendered against the Nusayri-'Alawites by Sunni sufi scholar Muhammad al-Maghribi (1764–1826), based in the Syrian city of Latakia.[12]

A contemporary fatwa cited on a jihadist Web site was made by Saudi cleric Hmoud bin 'Aqla' al-Shu'eibi in 2000 in response to general questions on the Nusayri-'Alawites and specifically on whether it was permitted to attend their weddings and funerals, and to pray for their dead. Al-Shu'eibi concludes that past scholars had deemed them to be "outside of the [Islamic] faith" and then quotes Ibn Taymiyya, especially in giving a political context for the historical alliance of the Nusayri-'Alawites with the enemies of Islam. He concluded that it is forbidden to attend their ceremonies or pray for their dead.[13]

Books hostile to Nusayri-'Alawites fall into two broad categories. The first stems from an Arab Nationalist line that stresses the non-Arab, specifically Persian, elements of their faith or the alleged Persian ancestry of the founders. The second is inspired by Wahhabi hostility to heterodoxy in general. The Iraqi government of Saddam Hussein, then in conflict with the Asad regime, hosted academic conferences in the 1980s and commissioned books to propagate the ethnic "otherness" of the Nusayri-'Alawites.[14] An example of a Wahhabi book, *Al-Nusayriyya,* that is readily available on several jihadist Web sites was authored by Saudi cleric 'Alawi bin Abdel-Qadir al-Saqqaf as part of a series attacking heterodox groups.[15]

Al-Saqqaf begins his tract by alleging that Nusayri-'Alawites believe they can accrue blessings by hurting Muslims. He also stresses the Persian origins of the sect and says that their hatred of some of the early companions of Muhammad is due to the latter's destruction of the Persian (Sassanid) Empire in 651 AD—an accusation hurled at Shi'as in general.[16] The book is a compilation of the origins, beliefs, and practices of the sect as understood from a fundamentalist Sunni perspective. It ends with a summary of all the attempts to rectify the "wickedness" of the Nusayri-'Alawites, all to no avail.[17]

FROM THREAT TO NUISANCE

To understand why textual incitement was important in the fourteenth century, and was rediscovered in the twentieth and twenty-first centuries, a brief overview of the circumstances of the Nusayri-'Alawites in antiquity up to modern times is necessary. Memories run deep in the Middle East and the historical narrative, real or imagined, informs the thinking and actions of Nusayri-'Alawites and their enemies alike.

The Nusayri-'Alawite creed was not borne out of resistance to orthodoxy but rather was a schism within schismatic heterodox groups. The death of the eleventh Shi'a Imam in 874 AD sent his followers into confusion over the validity of competing claims to the leadership of the sect. This centered on the inherited right of leadership of his infant son, who was later deemed to be the Mahdi in occultation, versus the claims to leadership by a brother of the deceased imam. The matter was complicated by the possibility that no infant was ever born, as the brother claimed. Then competing claims arose among the first faction, which later dominated, over who had access to the child in hiding, who had disappeared early into a cellar according to his loyalists, to emerge once again at the "end of times." What began as factionalism set in the alleyways of Baghdad and in the date plantations of southern Iraq soon migrated to northern Syria and the Levantine coast in the tenth century,[18] where a succession of Shi'a-friendly principalities allowed heterodox proselytizing, and the ideas consequently flourished and found mass appeal. This was also a time when Sunni orthodoxy was eclipsed; an Isma'ili Shi'a dynasty ruled in Cairo, and in Baghdad the Sunni caliph of the 'Abbasid dynasty owed his position to Shi'a generals. Sunnism was irrelevant, and the mantle of the leadership of the Shi'ite cause was up for grabs.

This period of heterodox consolidation in Greater Syria also witnessed Crusader incursions and the subsequent Sunni revival that quashed Shi'ism, checked Mongol attacks, and systematically drove out the Crusaders from their bastions. The Mameluke campaigns in Greater Syria, which shattered the Crusader Kingdom, and Ibn Taymiyya's fatwas were aimed at stamping out various heresies and solidifying the base of loyal support for orthodoxy and the central state. Every wave of Sunni attack—the last one being the Ottoman conquest in 1516 AD—seems to have pushed Nusayri-'Alawite families and communities from urban centers in Iraq and Syria into the relative sanctuary of the coastal mountains. This time around, it was Shi'a heterodoxy that was in eclipse.

For most of their history spanning four centuries in Greater Syria, the Ottomans dealt with the Nusayri-'Alawites as a banditry problem—a condition that could be tolerated as long as it did not drastically affect the state's ability to collect taxes. Chaos in the mountains never amounted to a coherent anti-Ottoman campaign due to the tribal and sectarian divisions among the Nusayri-'Alawites, something the Ottomans were aware of and promoted. One oral tradition has it that "the tribal divisions among us 'Alawites were invented by the mother of Sultan Selim."[19] Laying blame on the mother of the conquering Ottoman sultan is bizarre, but Selim was dreaded by the Nusayri-'Alawites as the man responsible for summoning and murdering thousands of their "notables" in Aleppo. This decapitation of the Nusayri-'Alawite communal and religious elite may have created a power vacuum that went un-filled for generations, and resulted in plenty of internal strife. In the mid-nineteenth century, the Syrian mountains were mired in a period of great chaos that had to be addressed by the central authority since it began affecting trade routes from Mediterranean ports to the cities of the Syrian interior. The Ottomans enacted policies of population control such as settling loyal Sunni tribes along the trade routes[20] and trying, once again, to bring Nusayri-'Alawites into the Sunni fold by rewarding the tribal leaders who yielded to its authority and pun-ishing those who didn't. The nuisance had de-veloped into a headache, and pre-emption was warranted to prevent Western intervention on behalf of the Nusayri-'Alawites, as other minority groups such as the Druze and Maronite Christians began to find patrons in Western powers.[21]

One last-ditch attempt to Sunnify the Nusayri-'Alawites was embarked on by Diya' Bey, Ottoman governor of Latakia from 1885–1892, through integration and religious re-education. But that effort, too, petered out and had no lasting effects.[22] Diya' Bey's efforts were seen as conciliatory by most Nusayri-'Alawite writers in the twentieth century, while others portrayed him as a bloodthirsty tyrant who casually puffed at his *nargilah* while watching impaled Nusayri-'Alawites die a slow death.[23]

The nineteenth century began and ended without the Sunnis taking much notice of the Nusayri-'Alawites. The Syrian branch of the nascent Salafi movement at the end of the nineteenth century and early twentieth century even began with attempts to find common ground with Shi'as—the Nusayri-'Alawites never factoring much into their discourse—in direct contrast with Iraqi Salafis, who felt threatened by Shi'a numbers and assertiveness in Baghdad.[24] In Syria, neither the Shi'as nor the Nusayri-'Alawites mattered much, and they certainly did not loom large in Sunni consciousness as a threat.

The period spanning the collapse of the Ottoman Empire after World War I and Syrian independence after World War II, during which the occupying French oscillated between carving out an independent state for the Nusayri-'Alawites and integrating them within Syria, marked a period whereby a new narrative for Nusayri-'Alawite identity was devised and developed. It was this narrative—one of Arab ethnic cohesion and re-integration into the Shi'a mainstream—that eventually succeeded against claims of a separate Nusayri-'Alawite identity pressed by the advocates for a separate Nusayri-'Alawite state.[25]

This process of conformity to Arabism and Islam was aided by conciliatory Syrian Sunnis, intent upon maintaining the territorial integrity—such as it remained after the amputation of Palestine, Lebanon, and Transjordan—of Greater Syria. A Nusayri-'Alawite insurgency against the French (1919–1921), one that started after the occupiers embroiled themselves in an internal sectarian war between Nusayri-'Alawites and Isma'ilis, quickly took on a nationalist tone, with limited logistical aid trickling in from Sunni nationalists in Damascus and Hama.[26] The more the Nusayri-'Alawites rejected sectarian particularism, the more they were rewarded by gestures of acceptance by Arab nationalists, such as the fatwa recognizing them as Muslims issued by Mufti Amin al-Husayni in July 1936.[27] Rather than issue fatwas condemning them as heretics and apostates, sympathetic Sunnis began authoring books highlighting the "true Arabness" of the Nusayri-'Alawites and the economic viability of their areas if properly developed, whereas in the past these regions wallowed in neglect and impoverishment.[28] Sunni Arab Nationalists sought to bring the Nusayri-'Alawites into the fold of the Syrian state. To this end, a new legacy of textual inclusion was formulated, and Ibn Taymiyya's words were forgotten, or dismissed.

~

BACK TO BEING A THREAT

This warm embrace into "Arabism" may have bred a false sense of confidence in a new generation of Nusayri-'Alawites. This confidence characterized the military circles especially, mobilized as they were with other marginal Sunni and sectarian blocs of recent peasant ancestry to overcome their inner sense of sectarian or class exclusion, and to fill the vacuum left behind by the weakened traditional power-players in Syria, the urban Sunni notables.[29] These outcasts—marginal Sunni and sectarian blocs of recent peasant ancestry—were also motivated and united by a desire for revenge against the urban Sunni notables. The notables were the principal landowners, and socialist-inspired land reallocation not only took away their economic viability, but empowered the very sharecroppers they had treated as nothing better than serfs— chosen by the landowners principally because, as marginal groups, they would be less prone to corporate assertiveness and to decrying their miserable conditions. The sons of the peasants

24

were serving up just desserts. Big changes were in the air, heady confidence was unleashed.

It was against this backdrop that groups of Nusayri-'Alawite, Isma'ili, and Druze officers began to vie for complete control through a military coup in the 1960s. Vigorous and determined, those who had come up in the ranks were faced with a Sunni elite enfeebled by the loss of its traditional leaders and by the community's traditional disdain for careers in the military. The Sunnis seem to have been taken by surprise, and were left in a temporary state of shock. Those vocally warning of a Nusayri-'Alawite takeover were likely to be members of other heterodox sects, who felt that they had missed an opportunity to seize power. Once they were sidelined, the rivalry was narrowed down to factions within the Nusayri-'Alawite camps, conclusively settling in favor of Hafez al-Asad in 1970.[30]

The Sunni response, when it came, was launched by the conservative reactionaries, the Islamists. They had been the rivals of the urban notables, drawing support from urban artisan classes. Thus, they were the only Sunni body left intact.[31] They found a new calling in agitating against and thwarting proposed changes to the constitution enacted in 1973 by al-Asad, whose outward motives were secular, but whose secret agenda, as portrayed by the Islamists, was the artificial ascendency of the Nusayri-'Alawites.[32]

The Sunni reaction soon turned violent. Nusayri-'Alawite officers, academics, and professionals fell victim to the assassin's bullet. At every stage, and with every violent clampdown by the regime, conciliatory Sunni Islamists were further dragged into the radical camp.[33] The radicalization within the Sunni Islamists was encouraged by the Jordanians and Egyptians, then at odds with the Asad regime, whose media organs employed blatant sectarian rhetoric.[34] It seemed to those fighting against the regime that victory was within reach. Even at this late stage, al-Asad was unwilling to think of the Islamists as a hostile behemoth and he held the view that most of them could be co-opted to accept his rule. This was seen by the other camp as irresolute weakness, confirming its sense of imminent victory. But an assassination attempt against the president in June 1980 and the release of the Islamist revolt's manifesto the following November—which brought the sectarian struggle into focus for the first time by directly threatening the Nusayri-'Alawites as a community and branding them as heretics[35]—seemed to have been a rude awakening for al-Asad, showing that there was no way to defuse the situation but to take it to its bloody conclusion.

The denouement came in February 1982 in the old city of Hama and lasted for several weeks. In a test of wills, the Syrian regime demonstrated that it would go to every limit to stay in power, even if it meant the destruction of a major city and the loss of tens of thousands of civilian lives. This time, it was the Islamists who were in for a rude awakening. The shock over what transpired in Hama effectively bought the regime a quarter century of peace, during which the Sunni merchant classes and some religious scholars were cultivated by the regime and co-opted, all while being closely watched for any signs of disloyalty by multiple Nusayri-'Alawite-dominated security outfits. Even the Muslim Brethren now opted for a conciliatory tone.[36]

THE FALL OF THE Saddam Hussein regime in April 2003 changed the dynamics of the Middle East, a region lulled into the complacency of a status quo that identified autocracy with stability. Autocrats across the region felt compelled to respond to this challenge. They were only distinguished by the severity of their hostility to the political changes in Baghdad, and in judging who would be the beneficiary of these changes when the regional balances, marked by Shi'a ascendancy in Iraq, were redrawn. An axis comprising Jordan, Egypt, and Saudi Arabia emerged to warn of a "Shi'a Crescent," an Iran-Iraq War-era scare tactic employed by the Iraqi Ba'athists to compel jittery Gulf Arabs to bankroll their war against the Ayatollah Khomeini regime in Iran. It was reanimated to describe an alleged secret Persian plan, centuries in the making, to span a territorial land mass from the Mediterranean to the Persian Gulf, one that would employ

Shi'a communities in a determined effort to control the natural resources of the Middle East.[37] Irrespective of its accuracy, it told a story, with names and addresses, of an Iranian-funded campaign, decades in the making, to turn Syrian Sunnis into Shi'as; it was all part of the "Shi'a Crescent" plan, banking on the popularity and iconography of Shi'a Hezbollah as a victorious redeemer of Arab and Muslim pride against the Zionists.[38]

The notion that this secret campaign was in the works meant that the standoff of Sunnis versus the Nusayri-'Alawite oppressors was not neutral and static, but rather one of long-term attrition in favor of the Asad regime. Once again, the Nusayri-'Alawites were portrayed as a threat to the survival of Sunnism in Greater Syria.

A 2006 study funded by the European Union, and supervised by a group of leftist Syrian oppositionists, concluded that the success of Shi'a proselytizing among Syrian Sunnis, although real and officially encouraged, was minimal and generally ineffectual, a conclusion that concurs with field inquiries made by this author.[39] However, its conclusions prompted a London-based group of Sunni Syrian oppositionists, who describe themselves as non-sectarian liberals, to commission a counter-study that accused the earlier one of being pro-Nusayri-'Alawite. It was published by the International Institute for Syrian Studies in April 2008 to provide an overview of the history of Shi'ism in Syria from 1919 to the present day, and despite its claim to objectivity it is saturated with a stringently anti-Nusayri-'Alawite tone.[40]

The later study is a watershed in the debate over the threat faced by Sunni Syrians, arguing that the rates of conversion were deliberately understated by the earlier study to minimize the extent of the challenge. Accuracy of numbers and statistics is not what matters here; a Sunni Syrian reading the 147-page report, well-researched and argued, would be left with the impression that his or her very identity, and the long-term survival of that identity, are at stake. Whereas Hafez al-Asad played things safe and always sought not to inflame Sunni sensitivities, his heir and successor since 2000, Bashar al-Asad, is not that deft, arrogantly allowing the

Shi'a proselytizing to proceed at a feverish rate. It is "totally natural," the tract asserts, to be concerned with the rise of Iranian influence in a country like Syria that lies at the confluence of three continents and shares borders with five countries of manifest political importance in the Middle East (Palestine/Israel, Lebanon, Iraq, Jordan, and Turkey). It is noteworthy that a tract commissioned by secular oppositionists would lend itself to do-or-die messianic fervor in its introduction, employing the very tone and terms of the jihadists:

> "From the religious angle, Syria . . . simultaneously occupies a highly sensitive position and religious stature for Sunni Muslims and the Shi'a sect, for the Sunnis view it as the fortified bastion of Islam, and they believe—based on religious texts—that it shall be one of the last fortresses of Islam (Sunni) if the Muslims are under pressure, while the Shi'as believe—in contrast—that it is the country where the oppression of Shi'as began since the emergence of their schismatic religious sect nearly thirty years after the death of the Prophet Muhammad . . . and on the other hand

most Sunnis believe that [the vicinity of Damascus] will witness the emergence of the Mahdi, while the Shi'as believe it shall be the land that will stand against [their] awaited Mahdi!"

A GLOBAL CALL FOR ARMS

One of the first calls to widen the jihad against the Nusayri-'Alawites beyond the immediate circle of Syrians came from the pseudonymous Abu Mus'ab al-Suri, a Syrian national who rose to the heights of renown in jihadist circles as a pre-eminent strategist and visionary of global jihad in the last five years.[41] Shortly after the death of Hafez al-Asad in June 2000, al-Suri published an extended essay[42] in which he addressed the survival of the Sunnis in Syria under the threat of Nusayri-'Alawite domination:

"A threat that places us [Sunnis] in Greater Syria before a fact in which . . . we either remain or disappear; do we and the [Sunnis] in Greater Syria remain as guardians of the religion of Allah in the blessed Greater Syria, or shall the heretical sects, comprising the Jews, the Crusaders, the 'Alawite Nusayris and the other deviating sects, remain in it."[43]

Al-Suri laments the fact that at al-Asad's death, the only recognizable opposition to Bashar's takeover came from within the Nusayri-'Alawite elite, and specifically from his estranged uncle and nephews, as well as former senior commanders of the military and security services.[44] Al-Suri infers that it was the decision of the "new Zionist-Crusader world order . . . that the 'Alawite Nusayri occupation and their control over the Sunnis of Syria and Lebanon should continue," while Sunnis were distracted by mercantile activity and menial aspects of daily life, all the while being humiliated in their own country.[45]

Al-Suri cites Ibn Taymiyya's fatwas in full to highlight the doctrinal basis for the alleged wickedness of Nusayri-'Alawites, which was exposed, in his eyes, once again by the petitions for secession from the Syrian state during the period of the French mandate. In his view, the

Ba'ath Party was founded by cunning thinkers drawn from 'Alawite and Christian ranks to be the political vehicle by which Nusayri-'Alawites would undermine the natural Sunni order of primacy. Once in power, the Ba'athists committed all sorts of travesties, such as giving up the Golan Heights to Israel and supporting the Maronites as they massacred Palestinians and Sunnis in Lebanon. The foremost task of the Nusayri-'Alawites in power is to "enable the Jews to control the region from the Nile to the Euphrates"[46] by several possible scenarios, all of which entail the destruction of Syria's military might and a program of financial and cultural liberalization that would weaken the Sunnis in Syria and make them more amenable to becoming slaves of "the Zionist-Crusader economy."

Most of the essay is dedicated to making a conventional case for jihad from a radical Islamist perspective. In summary, al-Suri argues that taking the life and wealth of the Nusayri-'Alawites is already sanctioned by Islamic authorities, and that it is incumbent upon every Muslim to fight them.[47]

Al-Suri berates the Sunnis of Greater Syria and asks, "Have you acquiesced to trade, to [university] degrees, to menial jobs, or to farming and the tending of cows, have you acquiesced to food, drink, travel and picnics, have you acquiesced to restaurants and resorts . . . ?"[48] Al-Suri demands that they renounce their indolent and cautious ways, and counsels that the easiest path to repentance is through jihad. He reveals that a nascent group of young Sunnis, both Lebanese and Syrian, had been plotting to fight the Nusayri-'Alawites and the Christians. However, their organization was uncovered by the fighting near Tripoli in early 2000 that was led by the Lebanese jihadist leader Abu 'Aisha against the Lebanese Army, which in turn was aided by Syrian expertise and military might.[49]

Al-Suri addresses "the jihadists in Egypt, the [Arabian] Peninsula, Kurdistan, Turkey, Iraq, Libya, Morrocco, Chechnya, Bosnia, and Afghanistan" and claims that it was from Syria in the early 1960s that jihad began against "the apostates and the seculars and Nusayri aggression," reaching its pinnacle in the 1980s. He declares that if the youth of Greater Syria make a move to reignite the jihad there, then "you should support and participate."[50] The jihadists, he says, should draw lessons from the past struggle by widening the base, not limiting it to a small vanguard. They should "highlight the essential [sectarian] identity of this confrontation with the 'Alawite Nusayris" by not clashing with the other sects, and by refraining from striking at the pro-regime Sunnis in its first phases, reverting to the tactic of assassinating Nusayri-'Alawites in majority Sunni areas.[51] The jihad, al-Suri advises, would be aided by disseminating the idea of the blessedness of Greater Syria, to rally fighters from all corners of the Muslim world.[52]

In a series of articles urging worldwide jihadists to take the fight to Syria, another influential jihadist ideologue, Abu Baseer al-Tartousi, summarizes a compilation of sayings and traditions attributed to Muhammad extolling the virtues of Greater Syria, especially in regard to Muslim regeneration when faced with external enemies.[53] The corruption of Greater Syria, induced by "the rule of the heretics of the age," the Nusayri-'Alawites, has reflected itself negatively on the general wellbeing of the Islamic *ummah* (community), he wrote, adding that Greater Syria's ascendance is a necessary component to the resurrection of a strong and vibrant Islam. It is for that reason, al-Tartousi argues, that Greater Syria has always been the target of invasions to weaken the religion. However, Islam's salvation shall come at the hands of a vanguard of Muslims from Greater Syria, and the vicinity of Damascus shall be the sanctuary of the believers, according to Muhammad.[54]

In a subsequent essay, al-Tartousi castigates the Nusayri-'Alawites as a sect outside the accepted doctrinal realms of Islam and the glory of Arabism, and adds that "[the Nusayri-'Alawite sect] can never be patriotic . . . or safeguard the safety and power of the realms of the Muslims . . . For I am one of those who has lived among and interacted with the Nusayris in their mountains and plains, and learnt their secrets, and their dangerous esoteric doctrines . . . the [loyalty] of the Nusayri is merely to his lusts and cravings, and he has no other [loyalty] but to that . . ." Al-Tartousi, as his pseudonym indicates, is from Tartous, a formerly mixed Sunni and Christian town surrounded by hills populated by Nusayri-'Alawites. Al-Tartousi warns that if the Nusayris should lose their control over the government in Damascus, then they will revert to a secret plan of secession, supported by the United States and the West as part of their policy to break up the lands of the Muslims. He addresses those concerned about Syria to immediately make plans for what comes after the collapse of Nusayri-'Alawite rule in Damascus.[55] For al-Tartousi, the fight does not end with the overthrow of the Asads, but must continue to deny the Nusayri-'Alawites the chance to regroup, indicating that more acute measures need to be taken to defuse the threat once and for all.

For decades, the Nusayri-'Alawites had sought doctrinal refuge and acceptance within the ranks of mainstream Shi'sim. Mainstream Shi'as, especially in Lebanon next door, happily obliged as rising Nusayri-'Alawite fortunes in

Syria translated into better circumstances for Lebanese Shi'as as well. It should be remembered that in 1973, when Lebanese Shi'a leader Musa al-Sadr issued his fatwa deeming Nusayri-'Alawites to be Muslims, Iran was still ruled by the Shah. In effect, the rise of Hafez al-Asad was the only manifestation of its kind at the time of Shi'a revivalism.[56] Nusayri-'Alawites needed the fig leaf of Shi'ism to inoculate them against the severe measures prescribed for their lot by medieval scholars such as Ibn Taymiyya, for even he never went as far as calling for the extermination of mainstream Shi'a laypersons; he called for killing the Shi'a elite only. But the jihad in Iraq changed all that. Abu Musa'ab al-Zarqawi argued that Ibn Taymiyya's hesitation to call for the annihilation of all Shi'as was inapplicable in the modern era, for in a democracy Shi'a laypersons choose to elect their elite, and hence are culpable as accomplices.[57] Thus, it matters little if Nusayri-'Alawites profess Shi'ism: they are all to be targeted.

After decades without any jihadist activity, a Syrian jihadist group announced itself on May

27, 2007, indicating that the sectarian nature of the regime was its chief rallying cry. The announcement came in the form of an audio recording allegedly made by the emir, or leader, of the new group, calling itself *Jama'at altawhid wel jihad fi bilad alsham* ("Monotheism and Jihad Group in Greater Syria"). The choice of the name "Monotheism and Jihad" indicated that the group drew its inspiration from al-Zarqawi, who started off in Iraq by using that name before aligning himself officially with Al-Qaeda. The emir of the new group, using the pseudonym "Abu Jandal," proceeded in a 43-minute speech to deliver messages to different constituencies inside Syria.[58]

Abu Jandal began by answering the question, "Who are we, and why do we wage jihad?"

"We are Muslim *mujahedin* from the blessed Greater Syria who are pained by the condition of our *ummah* that has languished under the Nusayri occupation for tens of years, and the Nusayris—who resent the Sunnis—are creative in desecrating the sanctities and the honor of the

Muslims under the cruel guidelines set down by the Nusayri [Hafez al-Asad] . . ."

Turning to the Sunnis of Syria, Abu Jandal asked, "You who are renowned for your bravery, generosity, pride, dignity, and poise, and the rejection of injustice, how do you accept to be ruled by the lowliest of creatures, the Nusayris, the Druze, and the haters?" He called upon them to rise up and "cut the limbs of the Nusayris and their necks, strike them down everywhere, for they are spread in every place to make it easier to hit them and to uproot them . . ." Following the advice of al-Suri,[59] Abu Jandal reached out to the Kurdish population of Syria. He bemoaned the regime's crackdown against Kurdish dissent, while "the new world order that is sponsored by America, the bearer of the Cross, and the great sponsor of unbelief" is silent, even though it claims to respect the rights of minorities. Abu Jandal played to the sympathies of the Sunni Palestinians and Syrians who ended up as refugees from Iraq, contrasting their fate and their flight from Iraq with the welcome that the Syrians had extended to the Lebanese Shi'a who had crossed the border to Syria during the war between Hezbollah and Israel in the summer of 2006.

However, he diverged from al-Suri's advice by taking a very harsh tone with Sunnis working for the security forces, warning them that since they "have turned Bashar, and before him his dead father . . . into a god . . . for [them] there will only be slaughter, then slaughter, then slaughter, at the hands of the youths of Islam." At a later point in the speech, Abu Jandal called the Ba'ath Party the "party of the devil that should be wiped clean out of Syria's great history." He also discussed at length the corruption of the inner circle and relatives of the Asad family.

Addressing Bashar al-Asad as "the dog of the Nusayris,"[60] Abu Jandal promised a "long, long guerrilla war" that "we have prepared for you and that you can't imagine." He claimed that Bashar had narrowly missed a "tight ambush" laid for him by the group the preceding April.[61] Abu Jandal asked Bashar mockingly, "Do you really think you will finish a second term?" The speech was released the same day as a presidential referendum that gave Bashar al-Asad another term of seven years as president. Abu Jandal also saluted an organization called Jund al-Sham as the pioneers of contemporary jihadism in Syria. However, save for a few terrorist acts attributed to them, such as the attack on the U.S. Embassy in Damascus in September 2006, little is known about their goals and ideology.[62]

The only other message attributed to Abu Jandal emerged on August 14, 2007, to eulogize the death of Lebanese jihadist leader Abu Hurayra, who died during the four-month-long hostilities between the Fath al-Islam jihadist faction and the Lebanese Army that began in May 2007. Jihadist groups were at first wary of Fath al-Islam and its leader, Shakir al-'Absi, but embraced them wholeheartedly during the bloody fight with the Lebanese Army on the outskirts of Tripoli. At the time when the confrontations began, it seems that al-'Absi had sent his son-in-law to establish contact with the jihadists in Iraq, but the latter was killed in a shoot-out with Syrian troops at the Syria-Iraq border. At one point in late 2007, al-'Absi managed to slip into Syria, and by February 2008 he had made contact with the leadership of the self-styled Islamic State of Iraq, which had launched what it proclaimed as its leading role in worldwide jihad.[63]

The first major terrorist strike inside Syria since the Sunni revolt of the early 1980s was conducted by supporters of al-'Absi on September 27, 2008. (It has been conjectured that this act occurred as retaliation for the alleged arrest of al-'Absi by Syrian security forces in August 2008, or as part of a coherent strategy to take the jihad to Syria.) A car bomb was detonated at a military checkpoint before reaching its target, and consequently there has been plenty of speculation as to what the target was meant to be. The likeliest target, given the destination of the vehicle and the location of the checkpoint, was the Seyyida Zeinab shrine, the most revered Shi'a shrine in Syria. If that indeed were the target, it would have been chosen to inflame sectarian tensions just as the jihadists set out to announce the emergence of their group.[64] A few weeks before the bombing, Bashar al-Asad publicly voiced concern over Sunni Islamist activity in northern Lebanon and the ongoing clashes between Sunnis and the small Lebanese Nusayri-'Alawite community there. He was concerned that these clashes would spill over into Syria.[65]

A distinguishing development in jihadist thought has been its attempt to conceive a strategy for global jihad. At the end of the day, the jihadists have a finite number of resources to draw upon: able operatives, funding, and recruiting pools. Strategic thinking is a hallmark of Zarqawism and its adherents. The old guard of Al-Qaeda never conceived of Iraq as a new and viable battleground, while al-Zarqawi did. The jihadist supporters of al-Zarqawi pushed the idea of "following the action," finding gaps and opportunities in their war against the strategies of the West to maintain stability in the region. The September 11, 2001, attacks in the United States exhibited tactical flourish on Al-Qaeda's part, but it was not clear whether it had a well-thought-out strategy for what came next. Al-Qaeda assumed that the United States and its Western allies would be cowed by the magnitude of the attacks, and would seek an accommodation with the jihadists. Osama bin Laden perceived America to be "a paper tiger" that would run away from confrontation, as it did in Somalia. He was wrong. As such, it is not enough for jihadists of the Zarqawist school to draw attention to the sectarian odiousness of the Syrian regime, a situation that has changed little for decades. They need to make a strategic, long-term case that would clinch the argument for dedicating limited resources to the fight in Syria.

The clearest case coming out of jihadist ranks to suggest that Syria should be the next battleground was made in July 2009 by the pseudonymous "Abul Fadhl Madhi" on the Al-Fallujah Islamic Forum, the main Web forum still standing at the time for jihadists. Although not much is known about Madhi—he only began posting articles under this name in late 2008, and had only 71 posts, a relatively low number, on Al-Fallujah by the time of the above article—yet his stature is such that he is identified as one of the "Leading Writers of the

Al-Fallujah Islamic Forums."[66] The novelty of this essay is that Madhi doesn't feel that it's necessary to make a jihadist case, grounded in Islamic doctrine, against the "heresy" of the Nusayri-'Alawites as many writers have done before him. In fact, Madhi never uses the derogatory term "Nusayris." Rather, Madhi seeks to place Syria within the larger context of the jihadist project in the region.

Madhi explains the timing of his essay as a "preliminary exploration of [regime change] in Syria in regards to the jihadist project as a whole." He begins by explaining the rationale behind the West's rapprochement with the Asad regime, even though it stands accused of international bad behavior, such as allowing terrorists to cross into Iraq, or assassinating Lebanese Prime Minister Rafiq al-Hariri. Madhi finds the Western rationale in a quote attributed to French President Nicolas Sarkozy in which he allegedly said, "We have to choose: it is either the [Asad regime] or the Muslim Brethren." Madhi explains that by this reference to the Muslim Brethren, Sarkozy means it is better to have tyranny in Syria than any form of politicized Islam. Consequently, Madhi infers that the West fears the ascendancy of the jihadists if the Syrian regime is overthrown. Forestalling such an event, and given what Madhi describes as an inevitable U.S. or Israeli strike at Iran, the West now seeks to wean Syria away from its alliance with Iran.

Madhi asks, "What is the strategic vision of the global jihadist movement regarding the position of Syria in the regional system and its delicate geopolitical location? Should Syria remain a potential conduit for reinforcements [to Iraq] or is it time, or nearly time, for a fundamental strategic change?"[67] Madhi proceeds to explain Syria's geopolitical importance given the historical ambitions of its stronger neighbors and regional actors: Turkey seeking to reclaim an Ottoman "backyard," the Saudis seeking to prevent an anti-Saudi axis in the "Fertile Crescent," and Syria playing the role of the "soft" front for Israel, so that the latter could focus on the harder front across from Egypt. In the 1970s, after Arabism was discredited, Hafez al-Asad was given the role of clamping down on Islamist dissent, using his loyal base of Nusayri-'Alawites. With the advent of the Islamic Revolution in Iran, al-Asad found it convenient to strike a special relationship with the Iranians, cemented by sectarian bonds, to thwart the emergence of Iraq as a strong regional power, one that may have encouraged Syrian Sunnis to cast their lot with Iraq.

Madhi argues that Hafez al-Asad handled the issue of Shi'a proselytizing carefully, especially its component of bringing back the Nusayri-'Alawites into the fold of mainstream Shi'ism. But Bashar allowed the alliance with Iran to proceed at full speed, to the point of disrupting the equilibrium that his father had maintained with the Egyptians and the Saudis, especially after the American invasion of Iraq in 2003 that toppled Saddam and dramatically changed the balance of power in the region. This prompted the realignment of Egypt, Jordan, and Saudi Arabia against the Syria-Iran axis, after the Shi'as made gains in Iraq and Lebanon, and Sunni acolytes of the Iranians (Hamas) penetrated into Gaza. Madhi concludes that what one has now is stalemate, for

the Shi'as could not find firm footing in areas
beyond their direct control, while the Sunnis in
their turn were unable to destroy the Iran-Syria
axis. The "unknown factor that could compli-
cate the clashing strategies," Madhi surmises,
"and which could at the opportune moment
overturn the entire scene, is the strongly pulsat-
ing jihadist movement in Iraq, despite the cruel
blows, and the potential jihad in Greater Syria,
whose power hasn't been revealed yet . . . The
question is about the next step."

Madhi explains that the jihadists placed great
energy and logistical effort into the Iraq front,
as it was the primary stage for war. But the
massive strategic interests for global powers in
Iraq, especially the oil interests, also meant that
these efforts were matched by an attempt by
world actors to undermine jihad there. This led
to a war of attrition between the jihadists and
the "Crusaders and their acolytes in Iraq" since
early 2007. In his view, the struggle in Iraq also
strengthened Iran, by allowing it to renegotiate
an anti-Taliban pact for Afghanistan and Pakistan with the West, and Syria, by giving it a role
in the stabilization of Iraq. However, Madhi

believes circumstances may cause a war between the West and Iran, while at the same time the West will find ways to save Bashar al-Asad's regime. This is the clearest indication in Madhi's eyes of the "crucial" strategic importance that Syria plays for the West, and consequently why the jihadists must follow the action there.

After making the strategic argument, Madhi explains why Syria will be easier to target than Iraq. Since Syria lacks natural resources, the West can't make a case for an expensive military campaign to intervene on behalf of the Asad regime. And given that the Sunnis are ruled by a minority of Nusayri-'Alawites, Shi'as and Shi'a converts, "who do not exceed a quarter of the population in the worst case scenario," regime change there can be built on "a solid popular ground, one that was never available at any time in Iraq." The demise of the Syrian regime or its "collapse into chaos" would immediately benefit neighboring Sunni blocs in Iraq and Lebanon by giving them strategic depth in Syria proper. Arms would no longer be sent overland to Hezbollah all the way from Iran, weakening the Lebanese Shi'as vis-â-vis the Sunnis, who equal them in numbers. The jihad in Iraq would be invigorated by a situation similar to that in Afghanistan, where the jihadists can rely on crossing the border into the relative refuge of Pakistan; in this case, the fight against the Americans can be sustained by giving safe haven for the Iraqi jihadists in Syria. Most importantly, "the jihadist project would get a direct confrontation with Israel, in an area ideal for guerrilla warfare, which is the occupied Golan Heights, without having to wage a costly struggle to overpass the Shi'a enclaves in Southern Lebanon."

The urgency for Madhi stems from the need to allow the Sunni masses in Syria to join the fights in Iraq, Lebanon, and Israel, and also because the process of Shi'a conversion, although numerically insignificant at this time, is expanding exponentially. Projections indicate that in twenty years around 500,000 Sunnis out of 30 million would convert. Madhi cites the aforementioned International Institute for Syrian Studies report to make his case.

Madhi wrote his essay with the detached tone of an analyst's memorandum addressed to the leadership of global jihad. He refrained from Islamic arguments or demagoguery. However, it is interesting to consider the feedback and debate among the rank-and-file jihadists and their sympathizers that ensued on the Al-Fallujah forum. One commentator who claims to be inside Syria asks how it is that the Sunnis can be mobilized when they have acquiesced to the humiliation which they endure and when the jihadist cells there have been dismantled by the regime. He adds, "I don't know any jihadist outside of prison and I live with the jihadists of the Internet, so how will the jihadist project recruit me or how will I get to the jihadist project?" Another commentator says that "if Syria is hit by Israel or the United States, only then will the jihadist project become energized as happened exactly in Iraq." Yet another commentator alerts Madhi that the occupation in Iraq created the conditions for a jihadist outbreak—conditions that are "hard to reach in a stable society that did not suffer an occupation" such as that of Syria. This same commentator adds that fighting the Israelis in a condensed area as heavily fortified as the Golan Heights is impossible, and that staging grounds along the long border with Jordan would be better suited for jihadist attacks against Israel. He also makes the point that the Iraqis were among the most highly militarily trained nations in the world due to the recurrent wars they have fought, and says that Iraqi society is intrinsically rebellious, violent, and willing to sacrifice for a cause, whereas Syrian society is quietist and careful, and less tribal. Furthermore, he writes, the Syrian state would marshal all its security services to nip jihadist activity in the bud, while in Iraq there was room for maneuverability and guerrilla tactics, implying that these conditions were borne out of the absence of a security state post-Saddam.

EXPRESSIONS OF SECTARIANISM

In an autocratic country such as Syria, where giving voice to sectarian differences is punishable by law, it is difficult to gauge the public perceptions of groups that differentiate themselves according to sectarian identity, whether Arab Sunnis, Nusayri-'Alawites, Druze, Christian, or Isma'ili. Certainly, there is no access to polling data or independent analytical research that sheds light on the relative acuteness or diffuseness of inter-sectarian antagonism. Coupled with a recent, and easily recalled, history of sectarian strife, notably the period of the late 1970s and early 1980s, such discourse is self-censored by the individual Syrian citizen to ward off scrutiny by the myriad security services keeping tabs on political loyalties. Hence, and as if by rote, outsiders asking about sectarianism in Syria are likely to be met initially by a barrage of regime-sanctioned talking points. These invariably revolve around the harmony of Syria's society, the rich diversity of its people, and the belief that any internal discord is due to foreign—colonial, imperialist, Zionist, etc.—meddling.[68]

However, there are times when a Syrian, for a variety of reasons, is willing to express inner fears or resentments concerning sectarianism. There is a dearth of such material, which under normal conditions would be reflected in press reports. In a country like Syria, where regular citizens assume that foreign journalists and their interlocutors are closely watched by the security services, and where foreign reporters are punished by withholding entry visas,[69] it is doubtful whether reporters can get straight answers on topics as sensitive as Nusayri-'Alawite, Shi'a, and Sunni relations. Such accounts are critical in discerning emerging trends in a closed society such as Syria's. In this section, I seek to contribute my findings and impressions as an additional resource to what we know about such trends. Over the course of five visits to Syria, traveling throughout the country, I have collected many anecdotes, quotes, and impressions about sectarianism, an issue that was foremost on my mind when exploring and researching in that country.

I will begin by describing a quest to find the tombs of two historical personalities with important symbolism for sectarian identity: Mu'awiya bin Abi Sufyan (602–680 AD), the founder of the Umayyad dynasty who along with his son are the most hated historical characters in Shi'ism, in Damascus; and al-Husayn ibn Hamdan al-Khasibi (873–957 AD), the effective founder of the Nusayri-'Alawi sect, in Aleppo.[70]

The locations of both tombs are kept secret by the two groups that revere them, to prevent desecration by adversaries. It is alleged that Mu'awiya's bones were disinterred and desecrated when the Umayyad dynasty was toppled in the eighth century, and it remained a tradition for Shi'as, even as late as the 1970s, to "go and urinate on Mu'awiya" when in Damascus. The Syrian government has "discovered" another tomb in the Bab al-Saghir cemetery for Mu'awiya, which also holds the remains of four other companions of Muhammad. The chief gravedigger at the cemetery volunteered that this is not Mu'awiya's real tomb, but would not go as far as giving its real location.[71] On a later visit to the cemetery, another gravedigger, a recent Sunni Arab refugee from Baghdad, recounted anecdotes of how Iranian pilgrims, visiting nearby Shi'a shrines, would pelt Mu'awiya's "fake" tomb at the cemetery with stones and strive to throw garbage through its barred windows. Indeed, the window panes at the tomb are all broken. "The *majus* threw stones

. . . they don't have a religion, we know this in Iraq," he told me. "The donkeys don't even know that Mu'awiya is not here." This is one instance of the transference of sectarian radicalism from Iraq and Iran that would naturally affect Syrian sensibilities.[72] Mu'awiya's alleged "real" tomb is in the Naqashat quarter, but residents of that quarter would be loathe to give outsiders directions to the tomb. I was led to it by over-eager children, who wanted to show off knowledge of their neighborhood. The adults I asked were circumspect and claimed that the tomb was in Bab al-Saghir. As it is, the tomb in Naqashat cannot be entered: it is part of a house, and the family living there can only grant entry into the tomb chamber if the visitor has a letter of authorization from the Ministry of Religious Affairs.

In Aleppo, I began asking about al-Khasibi's tomb at a Shi'a shrine. The Shi'a caretaker of the shrine said that al-Khasibi is "none of our concern. I was asked this question twenty years ago by a group who came from the [Syrian] coast"—a neutral, geographic term used by many Syrians when alluding to Nusayri-'Alawites—"and I didn't know back then, and I don't know now. You may find him near the al-'Aarabi shrine." Following the caretaker's advice, I went to the area pointed out to me, but the search was in vain. Finally, one informant remembered that "people from the coast" would secretly visit a shrine that lies within the nearby Hananu Barracks. He said this in a hushed tone, as if he was revealing a dangerous secret. When pressed about the name of the personage buried at the shrine and whether it was al-Khasibi, he claimed that he didn't know, but people call the saint there "Sheikh Yabruq" and that "he isn't visited by Sunnis."[73]

The following day, I went to the barracks, first built by the Ottomans. It now mostly serves as a military draft center for Aleppo's various neighborhoods, which is why I could enter dressed as a civilian without being asked my purpose at the gate. I had been told that the shrine lies at the farthest end of the barracks, and while trying to find my way, I stumbled into a military-only zone. A major in his early 40s motioned for me to come his way and asked me what I was doing there. I said I was trying to find al-Khasibi's shrine. The major, a

Sunni, also took on a hushed tone and began quizzing me about al-Khasibi and who he was. He had seen visitors arriving there, and they "looked as if they were from the coast," but he had never worked up the courage to ask to whom the shrine was dedicated. This was a Syrian Army officer serving at the barracks who played it safe by not asking his Nusayri-ʿAlawite colleagues anything about their faith, lest he be thought of as unduly preoccupied with sectarian issues, so he seized upon the arrival of a knowledgeable outsider to fill him in. After doing so, he gave me directions to the shrine, which is tucked away behind a late Ottoman-era sufi lodge. The shrine gate was locked, so I ducked into one of the recruiting offices and found another officer who I correctly identified, by his accent, to be a Nusayri-ʿAlawite. He was taken aback by my request to visit the shrine, and only relented after I said that I was a Nusayri-ʿAlawite from Iraq.[74] He took out a set of keys from his desk and ordered an orderly to open the shrine for me. Nothing at the shrine marks it as al-Khasibi's grave, and the only engraving mentions the benefactor who renovated it in 1954. When I returned with the keys, the officer counseled me not to tell anyone that this was al-Khasibi's tomb, and if asked, "tell them it is Sheikh Yabruq." Here was a Nusayri-'Alawite officer, a member of the ruling minority, speaking from within the confines of a military barracks, yet still afraid to reveal the location of the venerated shrine.

The following conversations about sectarianism are presented with minimal subtext. The validity and accuracy of the claims made are irrelevant: in civil strife, as opposed to a court of law, perception trumps reality. The speakers range from Nusayri-'Alawites invested in the regime to those who never left their mountain refuge for the jobs afforded to them by changed circumstances. It has been my experience that Sunnis are far more wary about airing their grievances. This is in contrast to the worried and profusely expressed views of the marginal sects, the Isma'ilis and Shi'as, who do not feel that they are beneficiaries of the regime, but would still constitute collateral victims in the case of a violent Sunni reaction against Nusayri-'Alawite rule. Their anxiety is probably accentuated by the fact that they live in mixed communities with the Sunnis, and their sectarian identity historically encourages a culture of impending doom and victimhood. My Druze interlocutors, whose views are not given here, see themselves as a community apart, a sense borne out of the remoteness of their population strongholds in the south of the country and an identity infused with a martial spirit. Also, they feel that the events in Lebanon, which pitted Shi'as against Sunnis, were not much of a concern since the Lebanese Druze had acted as allies of the Sunnis there. Given the sensitivity of the matter, and that these opinions were given in confidence, the names have been withheld. In some cases, where retribution by the Syrian security services is feared, biographical details are also limited.

I met a Damascus-born plastic surgeon, educated in Germany, whose father is one of the top officers of the Syrian Army and who was a close confidant of Hafez al-Asad. He has a picture of himself with the leader of Hezbollah, Hassan Nasrallah, prominently displayed at his clinic, along with pictures of his family; he should be the portrait of an assimilated upper middle-class Nusayri-'Alawite, confident of his standing in Syrian society. But he isn't. When he drives his late-model Volvo, he keeps a sub-machine gun handy on the passenger's seat. He said, "Do you know the Sunnis have a saying, *mal'oon baba Hassan* ('Cursed is Baba Hassan')? Do you know who Baba Hassan is? He's Ali bin Abi Taleb, the father of Hassan and the first of the twelve Shia Imams. They hate us. That is who they are . . . If given the chance, they will massacre us." The surgeon's family had assimilated into a more mainstream version of Shi'ism, opting to build a Shi'a mosque in its village, an act of piety to imply a closer affiliation to Islam. Clearly, the surgeon does not feel that any of that matters, since his family will never be accepted by Sunnis.[75]

One of the top security officers of the country refused to stray outside the official rhetoric when asked about the jihadist threat to Nusayri-'Alawites. "The strategic threat is Israel, and Al-Qaeda is a manifestation of that," he pronounced. When told that the jihadists view Nusayri-'Alawites as agents of the Zionists, and that the old official rhetoric against the jihadists seems to mirror jihadist motifs, he answered, "As a representative of the regime, I cannot let that accusation stand." When pressed, his standard answer, as if to reassure himself, was, "I cannot think like a sectarian; I will not take off the Arab Nationalist mantle. We have faced those terrorists before and we will face them down again . . . They killed the cream of our society, but we crushed them at the end."[76] Of the jihadists, this officer observed, "It is the same threat since 1975, it's all part of an Israeli design; we need to find strength in our Arab identity."[77]

The Nusayri-'Alawite rhetoric in the mountains is far more militant. "I am an 'Alawi and damn those who hide it," boasted a man in his mid-70s in the Abu Qobais valley. "Those Sunnis are the enemy. We have a saying: the enemy of your grandfather is not likely to be amiable to you." When asked whether he feared the jihadists, he boasted, "Let the Wahhabis, the enemies of Allah, show their heads and we will cut them off, again."[78]

A minor Nusayri-'Alawite religious functionary, who serves as one of several caretakers at the Nabi Younis shrine, one of the highest vantage points in the mountains, pointed to the mountain tops and the sea. "In case of an emergency," he said, "we have the mountain and the coast." (That is, if the regime falls in Damascus, then the Nusayri-'Alawites will secede.) "We cannot live with them," he said, pointing to the plains and hill-country to the east, meaning the Sunnis. "Aleppo, Homs, and Hama were all 'Alawite [cities], but they were all massacred." The 60-something sheikh recalled an anecdote: "A young Saudi sheikh once came up here, and he started railing against the pilgrims visiting the shrine. I punched him and pushed him down, leaving him with a cut above his eye. Later, his relatives came here to apologize, but they kept saying Wahhabi things. I told them that Abu Bakr, 'Umar and 'Uthman [the first three caliphs who followed Muhammad, revered by Sunnis and seen as usurpers by Shi'as] never converted to Islam. You should have seen their faces, the bastards."[79]

A conversation was relayed to me by a Sunni Syrian journalist who had been interviewing a Nusayri-'Alawite security officer living in an economically depressed neighborhood of Damascus. The journalist asked the officer where he was from. The officer, embarrassed by his poverty, replied, "I am ashamed to say where I am from." The journalist asked him, "Don't tell me you're from the president's town?" and the officer nodded yes.[80] One hears this lament often from Nusayri-'Alawites when one describes them as the ruling sect. They point out the poverty of their villages and the urban neighborhoods in which they congregate, and ask, "Is this the situation of a ruling sect? Only those at the top of the regime benefit, but we get the blame, and remain poor."[81]

A lower middle-class Sunni graduate student in Aleppo, whose family never likely kept any servants, disdainfully said, "The 'Alawites were our servants, but now some [Sunni] guys on campus take on the 'Alawi accent, a gruff accent, to show that they are connected to power."[82]

An upper-class Christian in the coastal city of Latakia observed that "the 'Alawites are no longer nouveau riche. They imitate the Christians and are influenced by the Lebanese fashion sense; they know the labels and what to buy." This is a far cry from the first half of the twentieth century, he said, when "no 'Alawites lived in the city. Even in the 1960s, when they were coming up in the world, my grandfather told me the story of an 'Alawite officer who sat in a sophisticated café here, and the staff would not serve him because he was an 'Alawite." Sectarian tensions in the city manifest themselves in muted ways: "The 'Alawites support one local soccer team, while the Sunnis support another." During celebrations, he said, "Alawites use their firearms, while the Sunnis wouldn't dare use anything but fireworks." He was visibly uncomfortable when talking about the subject, counseling me to "lower your voice when you use the word 'Alawites."[83]

Another comment came from a middle-aged manuscript dealer in Damascus, originally from Hamah, who described himself as an observant Sunni Muslim, but not a fundamentalist.[84] "Where are the real people of Damascus?" he asked. "What you see in the street is all riffraff. There will be a time when they get evicted and sent back to their mountains."

"It is the Shi'as who are biased and classify the Sunnis as infidels," responded an indignant

Sunni stamp dealer in Aleppo. "They are *bati-nis* [esoterics], all they do is secret. There are Shi'a families here in Aleppo who have pretended to be Sunni for centuries. They cannot be trusted. If they lose power, they will secede and they will make the city of Homs their capital. They have a secret plan to migrate to Homs and change the demographics there."[85]

Meanwhile, an Aleppine university professor of Kurdish extraction, who has carried a keychain bearing the face of Hassan Nasrallah for several years, lamented, "There was popularity for Nasrallah and Shi'as right after the [June 2006] war with Israel, but it evaporated when Saddam was executed [in December 2006]. People saw it as Shi'a revenge against Sunnis."[86]

"Salafis can't win in Syria, the nature of the culture here is too mild for such radical ideas," said a Sunni historian in a small provincial town who was accused of being a Shi'a convert, which he adamantly rejects.[87] One of his sons said that at first he used to visit a Shi'a shrine that was built in their town, but after being alerted to attempts to convert Sunnis to Shi'-ism, and after witnessing Saddam's execution, he still goes to the shrine but opts not to visit the revered Shi'a personality there. Rather, he visits another figure who is more acceptable to Sunnis.

A Sunni historian with ties to the regime went to great lengths to fudge the sectarian nature of the power structure and its ability to reform itself. He pointed out that Bashar al-Asad is married to a Sunni and that "he's raising his children as Sunnis," subtly indicating that the Nusayri-'Alawites at the helm of power can only be accepted in the long term by shedding their exclusionary sectarian identity and assimilating into Sunnism.[88]

"Jihadists won't find ground in Syria, and if they do, even I, an opponent of the regime, would rather have the Ba'athists than the Muslim Brethren," claimed a U.S.-educated businessman and self-professed sufi from a prominent family in Aleppo. "They are too radical for Syria and the chaos that happened in Iraq will be rejected as a price for overthrowing the regime."[89] A young Christian woman in Latakia said much the same: "Change means we become like Iraq."[90]

"No, the jihadists will succeed," retorted an Isma'ili leftist intellectual. "The regime has allowed them to take root. They allowed thousands of young men to fight in Iraq, and they still allow the jihadists to recruit and send money. It is the regime's own fault; they shut down all avenues for dissent and didn't allow change to happen gradually. If jihadists congregate, they turn a blind eye, but if liberals hold a meeting, then all hell breaks loose."

An Isma'ili schoolteacher, also a leftist, listening to the conversation added, "I see it daily, the sectarianism. The [Sunni] Bedouins are calling us infidels, and there are more of them than us. You see more women wearing *hijab*, you see more people at mosques. People are turning to Islam more and more, and you saw what they did when the Danish cartoons came, and the regime is allowing this to happen."[91]

A Syrian mob had set fire to the Danish Embassy in Damascus in February 2006 in retaliation for cartoons published in a Danish newspaper lampooning Muhammad. The Aleppine graduate student said shortly afterward, "Burning buildings is uncivilized, but we had to overreact so that they would not do it again."[92] A Danish student studying Arabic in Damascus observed, "The overreaction makes sense, it is the only type of expression they are allowed to have." He also alerted me that the anti-Danish campaign was orchestrated by a regime-sanctioned public relations company called Al-Mostaqbal.[93] The Danish Cultural Institute in the old city of Damascus felt compelled to put up a cloth banner outside its office at the time saying, "The manager and staff of the Danish Institute decry and condemn what Danish newspapers published in regards with the master of the universe, Muhammad . . ."

Referring to the young men who went to fight in Iraq, a traffic policeman asserted, "They are all holy martyrs."[94] The traffic of fighters has slowed down, observed the owner of a concession stand on the desert road to Palmyra, which also leads to the Iraqi border. "The regime has clamped down in the last year," he said, adding, "The Shi'as in Iraq kill any Syrian they find, even if he is a truck driver, just because he is Sunni."[95]

"Converting Sunnis to Shi'ism is being done by the brother of Rustem Ghazaleh," insisted a Sunni journalist in Damascus, thus ascribing such efforts to a much-hated Sunni figure of the regime, who is widely seen as corrupt and servile to the Asads.[96] "They target the country-side, because people there are more ignorant, but almost all of the Wahhabis who are getting caught and sentenced, and who I hear about, are from the countryside of Damascus, Aleppo, Idlib, and Dera'a. So the radicalism is also coming out of there."[97]

For all the attention and passion surrounding the claim of Sunnis converting to Shi'ism, the phenomenon remains a marginal one. One source from a village often cited as one of the first manifestations of Shi'a conversions in Sunni areas put it this way, "Only twelve of us pray at the Fatima al-Zahra' Mosque here. During the 'Ashura festival, the security officers monitoring us outnumber the worshippers . . . In the 1960s, a man here called al-Ghifri converted to Shi'ism. He was a hard and rude man who alienated many people on a personal level, but the Iranians gave him a lot of money. He only managed to convert some of his relatives, and here we are." They are alert to the rising wave of Sunni fundamentalism in the countryside: "The Salafis targeted a Christian church in the vicinity not too long ago. They threaten us. They hate us."[98]

"The regime is our only protection," lamented a middle-aged engineer from the historically Shi'a village of Nubbul, northwest of Aleppo. "There is tight control for now, but once it goes loose, then the terror will break out. There is plenty of money for it . . . Weapons are easy to circulate; smuggling even occurs across the Israeli border, so it shall be easier over the Lebanese and Iraqi borders . . . The population is backward, if a preacher stood up in Bab al-Faraj [in Aleppo] and railed against the Shi'as, then hundreds would gather around him, but if the same thing happened in the West they would laugh at him." Commenting on the rising radicalism of the countryside, he revealed that "a nearby village renamed itself Fallujah (after the Sunni city in Iraq that witnessed a bitter battle between the jihadists and U.S. troops) and put up signs to that effect. The government took down the signs. In another village, there was recently a shooting standoff with jihadists [and Syrian security forces] that lasted for four hours, and it never got reported in the press." Expressing concern on the deep-rootedness of sectarianism, he cited an example during the Lebanon war. "We had 1,450 Shi'a Lebanese refugees swarm into Nubbul, which is very poor. We went soliciting donations from the head of the Aleppo Chamber of Commerce who is also a member of parliament. You know what he asked us? He asked whether we Shi'as curse the companions of the prophet. He said that some Aleppines came to him and warned him not to donate because we the Shi'as curse the caliphs. This was a Ba'athist member of the regime saying this . . . Even the highest-ranking Sunni Ba'athist dreams of a Sunni takeover, since they are now afraid and humiliated by even the lowest-ranking 'Alawi security officer."

Sighing at the deep-rootedness of the situation, he revealed: "When my father and grandfather used to go to Aleppo, they would be pelted with potatoes. The Sunnis are embittered, and if given a chance now they will hurl knives at us, but they are afraid of the regime . . . They say we are the internal Jews. There will be a bloodbath, again."[99]

IMPLICATIONS FOR POLICY

These samplings of embittered sentiments do not mean that any of these people will pick up arms sometime soon. They do, however, capture an increasingly dominant narrative of sectarianism among Syria's population that could signify that those expressing such sectarian frustrations and fears would not stand in the way of either jihadists fighting against the regime, or the regime fighting back.

That said, one should not make too much of frustration. It is a phenomenon one encounters often in the Middle East. It hardly ever means that revolution is imminent. The markets are humming and, as the jihadists and their sympathizers acknowledge, most of the Sunni mercantile class, which in Syria accounts for a large section of the urban landscape, seems content with how things work in their country. But important socio-economic changes in that landscape have occurred during the past three decades, as the sprawl of cinderblock slums around Damascus can attest, blighting the city's former grandeur. Whereas the Sunni Islamist revolt of the 1970s and 1980s drew its strength from an urban artisan class, these slums are swelling with newcomers to the city—migrants whom the new jihad seeks to recruit—who left a rural scene of dwindling crop yields and exploding numbers. The angry young men, idling their days away in the gray concrete alleyways waiting for their luck to change, do not share a class enemy with the Nusayri-'Alawite peasantry, as their fathers and grandfathers once did in the 1940s and 1950s when they were united against the Sunni notable and landowner class. Another trend that I discerned during my travels was an increasing crime rate, some of which seems to be organized and abetted by corrupt security personnel. Alleviating poverty is highly unlikely in a "kleptocracy" where only a tiny sliver of the population can afford the $900 shoes on display at boutique shops around the Four Seasons Hotel of Damascus, while the vast majority of the population sinks deeper into misery. Some of the conversations presented above highlight the incubation of radical Islamism in the hard-pressed countryside. How will this wrath be dissipated? Or where will it be channeled?

The Obama administration has signaled in word and deed that a policy change is in the offing, a change that would accommodate the Syrian regime and normalize relations with it. The policy is bolstered by a chorus of apologists among analysts and academics, who maintain that the notion of autocracy being a guarantor of stability is back in vogue after the Bush years. The Syrian regime, the thinking goes, is as good as it gets for keeping simmering tensions under a tight lid. However, the change being considered is a bit of a gamble, and it is premised on the belief that the jihadists are now a spent force. An idea going around has it that the jihadists have delegitimized themselves by their extremism—their brand of fury now associated in the public mind with pointless chaos and mayhem—and are rejected as such by "stable, peaceful" autocratic societies such as Syria's. This could be a case of the dangers of believing one's own propaganda, for it overlooks the fact that the jihadists don't see themselves as contenders in a popularity contest; they are a vanguard, an elite, of Islamic redeemers who are out for revolutionary change, the kind of change that can't be brought about by winning elections. Their public image only concerns them as far as it impedes their ability to recruit talent and raise money. We must keep in mind that a jihadist sympathizer is by instinct a revolutionary nihilist, rather than a law-abiding citizen. Directing mayhem and chaos against the established order is exactly what draws him to the fight as a foot-soldier, and as an empowered and vengeful individual.

One important lesson that should have been learned from Iraq is that the fast-changing dynamics of the Middle East often outpace Washington's quick-fix policies. Engaging Syria may have made sense during the Clinton era when matched with the unchallenged stability of Hafez al-Asad's reign. But it makes little political and strategic sense to do so at this time. Projecting what may change tomorrow, and keeping in mind the state of flux still reverberating through the Middle East, must inform how new policies are made.

The jihadists will understand U.S. engagement with Syria as an ironic twist of events: rather than punishing the Syrians for enabling jihadists in Iraq, as publicly claimed by the Iraqi leadership, the Syrian regime would be propped up as a bulwark against jihadist expansion. In this Faustian deal, the jihadists smell weakness and opportunity. It remains to be seen whether they shall place their bets and limited resources on the chance that Syria would be a new battlefield that is conducive to jihad. In Iraq, the Zarqawists found that sectarian antipathy was a quick-burning fuel for their ideological machine—it was an innovation, and a leap forward, for jihadist strategy. The conversations above demonstrate that there are ample reserves of raw sectarianism in Syria that the jihadists may draw upon.

To borrow a gambling term, the jihadists arguing for action in Syria believe that they have hit the trifecta: in the Syrian regime, they have an enemy that is at once tyrannical, secular, *and* heretical. One, Syria is a hereditary autocracy; two, the Ba'ath Party is aggressively secular; and three, the Nusayri-'Alawites are beyond the pale of Islamic orthodoxy, adding insult to injury by "occupying" a sacred Sunni capital. In addition to that, the Syrian regime is perceived to advance U.S. and Israeli interests in the region, according to dominant jihadist narratives. These are all powerful and inspirational recruiting devices for the jihadists.

Furthermore, the jihadists, unlike their Iraq campaign experience, are aided by logistical familiarity with the terrain and customs of Syria; at the beginning of summer, one is always struck by the throngs of young Saudi, Kuwaiti, and other Gulf males—usually the best regional recruiting pool for jihadists—patiently waiting for their passports to be stamped at Syrian overland border points. Tens of thousands of them go there annually. At least tens of thousands may have Syrian mothers, married off to wealthier Saudis and Gulf Arabs who had gone shopping for younger brides. Plus, there are also tens of thousands of Sunni Syrian families residing and working in Saudi Arabia whose sons and daughters have been exposed to a Wahhabi curriculum, in many cases a sure recipe for radicalization. They too can be recruited. None of this familiarity or "pollination" with radical ideas was readily available in Iraq. Moreover, hundreds, if not thousands, of Syrian youth have been battle-hardened at the Iraq front after flocking to fight the U.S. invasion from the very beginning,[100] and later joining the Zarqawist insurgency. Many of them became mid-level leaders of the Al-Qaeda organization there. Some of them even became al-Zarqawi's most trusted aides.

Jihadists have been managing and carrying out logistical operations in Syria for years, constructing networks of safe houses, and figuring out which Syrian security officers can be bribed and which ones display talents that may be employed against them. While this know-how was originally devoted to sustaining the jihad in Iraq, it could easily be flipped toward a Syrian focus. Talented officers may be conveniently marked for assassination, denying the regime its most able enforcers. The bribable ones can be co-opted. The idea that a security regime can tether down the wild beast of jihadism misses the technological, financial, and recruiting innovations that have freed jihadists to a large extent from their past reliance on state sponsors. This newfound confidence accentuates the unwillingness of the "vanguard" to submit to any master beyond its revolutionary passions.

If the jihadists are not a spent force, and if they choose to focus on Syria, then it stands to reason that the Syrian regime may face a very grave challenge to its survival. With such odds, does it make sense to bet on the Asads at this time? Clearly, stability is not served by allowing the jihadists to have their way. But neither is it served by rescuing a regime built on unsteady, unpopular foundations, thereby rewarding all it has done to enable the jihadists in Iraq. Perhaps the regime may be reformed peacefully, allowing for transition to a legitimacy underpinned by elements other than brute force. The Asads have long survived on this sort of wishful thinking by the West, but the advocates of accommodating the Syrian regime don't have much to show for it in terms of tangible changes of behavior. Does economic liberalization, as enacted by the Asads, eventually lead to political liberalization? Is it possible to liberalize a power structure that hinges on allocating the largest share of Syria's economic opportunities to the Nusayri-'Alawite and Sunni loyalists of the regime? Does the regime want to reform? Can it reform without a slide into chaos? The regime has a proven record of stifling internal dissent, but is it a match for talented, globalized terrorists migrating to its cities and villages, hell-bent on waging jihad?

There are no convincing and straightforward answers to these questions. Syria is important, and it poses a strategic conundrum. It has been the purpose of this paper to demonstrate that

the global jihadist movement may further com-
plicate the situation. There are no daily head-
lines reporting on systematic bombings and
assassinations coming out of Syria, yet. However, the math that we can do is that jihad in
Syria makes strategic sense for the jihadists,
and as we have seen in Iraq and beyond, they
are rational and strategic actors who will follow
what is in their best interest. So the play in
Syria unfolds, and the bet on accommodating
that regime seems based, at best, on uncertain
grounds and is perhaps an exercise in wishful
thinking.

NOTES

1. Quote attributed to a high-ranking Christian Syrian official in the early 1990s, said at a private gathering, conveyed to the author by an attendee.

2. Cited in Hanna Batatu, "Syria's Muslim Brethren," *MERIP Reports*, No. 110 (November/December 1982), p. 13.

3. The case was first made by the author in "The Perfect Enemy," *The New York Sun*, July 1, 2007.

4. A promising and fuller examination of this topic is to be expected in the new book by Yaron Friedman, *The Nusayri-Alawis: An Introduction to the Religion, History and Identity of the Leading Minority in Syria* (Leiden, the Netherlands: Brill Academic Publishers, 2009).

5. For a full text of the fatwa, followed by a Nusayri-'Alawite rebuttal, see Muhammad Ahmad 'Ali, *Al-'alawiyoun fil tareekh, haqa'iq wa abateel* (Beirut: 1997), pp. 175–184. An abridged version of the fatwa aimed at a jihadist audience is available at http://www.tawhed.ws/r?i=xrkegb6j.

6. Nusayri-'Alawite popular traditions preserve the story of a "popular uprising" against the Crusader knights of the Castle of 'Arimah, in the plains southeast of Tartous. It began when the lord of the castle, identified as "Reem Hanna" in the Nusayri-'Alawite account, seduced the daughter of Rashid Aboli, who went on to cleanse his sullied family honor by launching an insurgency. The event is not clearly dated, but it is alleged that

it lasted until the castle was retaken by Noureddin Zenki, a Muslim commander from the mid-twelfth century. See Sarim Mahmoud Salih, *Al-ta'areef bil turath al-sha'abi*, undated, pp. 31–39. It should be noted that Muslim travelers during that era have commented on the relatively good treatment of Syrian Muslims by the Crusaders. See Ibn Gubayr's account in Robin Fedden, *Syria: An Historical Appreciation* (London: Robert Hale Ltd., 1956 [1946]), p. 171.

7. Friedman makes the case that the "first fatwa" was written much later after this Mameluke campaign but the account is unconvincing. Friedman correctly points out the confused nature of the "first" fatwa, in which Ibn Taymiyya lumps the Nusayris in with the Isma'ilis and mixes up their tenets. However this confusion could be further indication of Ibn Taymiyya's early, and uncertain, understanding of Nusayri-'Alawite doctrines, which are more accurately rendered in the later two fatwas. See Yaron Friedman, "Ibn Taymiyya's Fatawa against the Nusayri-'Alawi Sect," *Der Islam*, Vol. 82, Issue 2, pp. 349–363. It seems that Ibn Taymiyya had also written elsewhere about the Kisrawan campaign, which a Nusayri-'Alawite source identifies as the resolution of a dispute between the people of Kisrawan and the Tanoukhis of the coast, and confuses mainstream Shi'as with Nusayri-'Alawites. See Ahmad Hassan and Hamid Hassan, *Al-muslimoon al-'alawiyoun fi lubnan* (1989), pp. 121–145.

8. Nusayri-'Alawites would volunteer that Osama bin Laden's mother is one of their own, and so is his first wife (she's his first maternal cousin). This claim has been repeated by bin Laden's western biographers, but it remains far from being conclusive as it is attributed to a couple of press reports from late 2001. The Al-Ghanim family of the countryside of Latakia, who are bin Laden's maternal uncles, could very well be Sunnis as they claim: they originate from villages and hamlets to the immediate east and northeast of Latakia that are populated by Sunnis. There are at least two Nusayri-'Alawite families in Syria called Al-Ghanim, one of which originates from the Adana region in Turkey.

9. Arabic text available at http://www.tawhed.ws/r?i = 5zcwvuga.

10. Also Friedman, "Ibn Taymiyya," p. 357. For more on the 1317 rebellion and the reasons behind it, see Sato Tsugitaka, *State and Rural Society in Medieval Islam: Sultans, Muqta's and Fallahu* (Leiden, the Netherlands: Brill Academic Publishers, 1997), pp. 162–176.

11. Arabic text available at http://www.tawhed.ws/r?i = 6wr6by0e.

12. Dick Douwes, "Knowledge and Oppression; The Nusayriyya in the Late Ottoman Period," *La Shi'a Nel l'Impero Ottomano* (Rome: Actes du Colloque de l'Academie de Lincei, 1993), pp. 164–165. The actual text of the fatwa seems to have been lost to Sunni sources, and a conversation with the sheikh assigned to oversee al-Maghribi's mosque and tomb in Latakia (his name refers

to his immigration from Tunis to Syria) on May 10, 2007, revealed that the body of al-Maghribi's fatwas are not included in the manuscripts attributed to him, now held in Damascus. The only printed resource on al-Maghribi in Arabic makes no mention of his relations with the Nusayri-'Alawites. See Abdul-Fattah al-Adib al-Mahmoudi, *Kitab nukhbet al-akhyar fi manaqib al-qutb al-shaheer Muhammad al-Maghribi al-Nassiri* (1924 [1975]). It is interesting that of all the names of the accursed mentioned in a Nusayri-'Alawite collection of psalms (Kitab al-majmu'), al-Maghribi is the only person referred to beyond the thirteenth century as one of the enemies of the Nusayri-'Alawites. See Heinz Halm, *Al-ghinossiyah fil Islam* (Cologne, Germany: 2003, translated from German), p. 240. *Kitab al-Majmu'* is known as the *al-Dustoor* in Nusayri-'Alawite sources, and it is attributed to al-Maymoun al-Tabarani, an eleventh-century figure credited with propagating the Nusayri-'Alawite tenets in the Syrian coast. See Abu Musa and Sheikh Musa [al-Tartousi], *Rasa'il al-hikmeh al-'alawiyyeh*, Vol. 1, Diyar Aql (2006), p. 8, n. 1. It seems that names such as Ibrahim al-Dasouqi (thirteenth century) and al-Maghribi (nineteenth century) were added by later scribes.

13. Arabic text of the fatwa available at http://www.tawhed.ws/r?i=kcebwhca.

14. One anti-Nusayri-'Alawite book inspired by this line seems to be Suheir al-Feel's first volume, *Al-nusayriyyah*, which was published in Cairo in 1990. The Egyptian author is accused by a Sunni Syrian writer of relying

too heavily on the findings of a politicized academic conference held by the Shari'ah College of Baghdad University in 1985. See Muhammad Abdel-Hamid al-Hamad, *Ikhwan al-safa wel tawhid al-'alaw*, (Raqqa, Syria: 1998), p. 135. There does seem to be some limited Persian influence on Nusayri-'Alawism, especially regarding the celebration of some holy days, but most of it relates to the early period of the sect's incubation in southern Iraq before its migration to Greater Syria. See Meir Michael Bar-Asher, "The Iranian Component of the Nusayri Religion," *Iran*, Vol. 41 (2003), pp. 217–227.

15. 'Alawi al-Saqqaf is the proprietor of the *Al-durrer al-sunniyah* Web site, http://www.dorar.net. His work on the Nusayri-'Alawites (undated) can be found at http://www.tawhed.ws/r?i = q4md7mbs.

16. Al-Saqqaf, *al-nusayriyyah*, p. 39.

17. Al-Saqqaf, *al-nusayriyyah*, pp. 42–43.

18. For a compilation of the limited resources on these Shi'a-leaning principalities on the Levantine coast, see Hashim 'Uthman, *Tareekh al-shi'a fi sahil bilad al-sham al-shamal* (Beirut: 1994).

19. Conversations, Abu Qobais, July 4, 2007, and Jobel Birghal, July 5, 2007.

20. An example would be the Dandashi tribe that was settled along the vital trade routes linking Tripoli to Hama and Damascus as a defensive measure against Nusayri-'Alawite raiding bands. See Ahmad Wasfi Zakariya, *'Asha'ir al-sham* (Beirut: 2005 [1983]), p. 483.

21. The upheaval among Nusayri-'Alawites in the nineteenth century, so important in forming their approach to state power in the twentieth century, is beyond the scope of this paper. Important contemporary accounts of this period exist, notably Frederick Walpole, *The Ansayrii, and the Assassins, with Travels in the Further East in 1850–51 including a Visit to Nineveh*, Vol. 3 (1851, undated reprint) and Samuel Lyde, *The Asian Mystery: Illustrated in the History, Religion, and Present State of the Ansaireeh or Nusairis of Syria* (London: 1860 [and Boston: Adamant Media Corporation, 2005]). See also Stefan Winter, "The Nusayris before the Tanzimat in the eyes of Ottoman provincial administrators, 1804–1834," *From The Syrian Land to the States of Syria and Lebanon*, ed. Thomas Philipp and Christoph Schumann (Beirut: Orient-Institut der DMG, 2004), and Yvette Talhamy, "The Nusayri Leader Isma'il Khayr Bey and the Ottomans (1854–58)," *Middle East Studies*, Vol. 44, No. 6 (November 2008), pp. 895–908.

22. Douwes, "Knowledge and Oppression," pp. 167–168.

23. Muhammad Hawash, *'An al-'alawiyeen wa dawletahum al-mustaqilla* (Casablanca, Morocco: 1997), p. 161.

24. David Dean Commins, *Islamic Reform: Politics and Social Change in Late Ottoman Syria* (New York: Oxford University Press USA, 1990), pp. 84–88.

25. This period and these trends are well presented in Kais Firro, "The 'Alawis in Modern Syria: From Nusayriya to Islam via 'Alawiya," *Der Islam*, Vol. 82, pp. 1–31.

26. A reasonable account of the insurgency led by Salih al-'Ali in light of Nusayri-'Alawite oral traditions and French documents from the period can be found in Hawash, *'An al-'alawiyeen*, pp. 99–171.

27. Firro, "The Alawis in Modern Syria," p. 24.

28. The clearest representation of this Arab Nationalist genre was authored in 1946 by a Sunni civil servant who had been an administrator in the Latakia area. See Munir al-Sharif, *Al-muslimoon al-'alawiyoun, men hum wa ayna hum* (Beirut: 1960 [1946]).

29. The Sunni notable class was a relatively recent formation at that time, emerging from the post-Tanzimat land reforms, economic integration with Europe, the aftermath of an Ottoman retaliation against the instigators of anti-Christian riots in 1860, and as a reaction to the emergence of the CUP (Committee of Union and Progress) as the main power brokers in Istanbul. For an in-depth study of this class, see Philip Khoury, *Urban Notables and Arab Nationalism: The Politics of Damascus 1860–1920* (Cambridge: Cambridge University Press, 2003 [1983]).

30. This period is ably covered by Nikolaos Van Dam, *The Struggle for Power in Syria: Sectarianism, Regionalism and Tribalism in Politics 1961–1978* (New York: I.B. Tauris, 1979).

31. The urban notable class had its component of religious notables, or families that had dominated the religious establishment for several generations back, of all types of religious inclinations. But this component was hobbled by reforms enacted in 1949 that denied them control of religious endowments. For the development of Islamist politics and the emergence of the Muslim Brethren as the forerunners of this trend from the 1940s until the 1963 coup, see Johannes Reissner, *Al-harakat al-islamiyyah fi souriya min al-arba'eenat and hata nihayet 'ahd al-shishekli* (Beirut: 2005, translated from German). Reissner's account shows that the Islamists didn't pay too much attention to a perceived sectarian threat during this period. But it is noteworthy that Latakia had a highly active branch of the Muslim Brethren relative to other places in Syria, which could be an indicator that the Sunnis there, surrounded by Nusayri-'Alawites, found an early expression of a corporate identity under siege by flocking to politicized Sunni Islam, pp. 145–146.

32. See Abdel-Rahman al-Haj, *Dhawahir al-islam al-siyasi wa tayyaratuhu fi souriya, isti'adet al-khayyar al-dimoqrat* (2006), available at http://www.forsyria.org/arab/papers_full.asp?id = 12. Al-Haj makes the case that politicized Islam in Syria always conformed to non-violent expression, but the regime's violent overreactions in Hama in April 1964 and Damascus in 1965–67 encouraged radical Islamists on the fringe such as Marwan Hadid to call for a response in kind. Hadid had gone to

Jordan to join the guerrilla fighting against Israel, but was ejected from there as a result of the September 1970 war. At the time of the 1973 constitutional crises, Hadid advocated for an armed struggle against the regime but the Muslim Brethren stood firmly against him. Hadid's arrest in 1975 and death in prison the following year gave the radical Islamists a martyr figure that inspired them to conduct assassinations against Nusayri-'Alawite figures. Al-Haj set the killings of Nusayri-'Alawite cadets at the Aleppo Artillery College on June 16, 1979, as the beginning of the Islamist revolt. A hagiographic jihadist's account of Hadid is available at http://www.tawhed.ws/r?i = utd8ts28.

33. The history of the 1976–1982 revolt and its sectarian nature are best captured in Chapters Seven and Eight of Nikolaos Van Dam, *Al-ssira' 'ala al-ssulta fi souriya* (Arabic electronic version, 2006), available at http://www.nikolaosvandam.com/BOOKS%2020071201:%20 FIRST_AUTHORISED_ARABIC…INTERNET_EDI TION_OF_AL-SIRA%27_%27ALA_AL-SULTAH_FI …SURIYA..pdf. The transition in ideological terms from a peaceful to a militant Islamism is evident in the works of Sa'id Hawwa, one of the principal exiled Syrian Islamist ideologues of that era. He argued that the current regime must be understood in terms of apostasy but that the inevitable jihad against it must undergo a period of measured preparation, including the enlistment of observant Sunnis into the armed forces to gain military and strategic talents. See Itzchak Weisman, "Sa'id Hawwa

and Islamic Revivalism in Ba'thist Syria," *Studia Islamica*, No. 85 (February 1997), pp. 151–153.

34. For Egyptian and Jordanian sectarian propaganda, see Van Dam, *Al-ssira' 'ala al-ssulta*, pp. 134–135 and 153.

35. The manifesto, in its section directed to the Nusayri-'Alawites, calls upon them to rein in the audacity of the al-Asads. For the text of this section see Van Dam, *Al-ssira' 'ala al-ssulta*, p. 155. See also Hanna Batatu, "Syria's Muslim Brethren," pp. 12–36.

36. Even the Muslim Brethren recalibrated their political program to be more conciliatory and "democratic" in December 2004. See Al-Haj, *Dhawahir al-islam al-siyasi*, pp. 30–31. The current leader of the Muslim Brethren, Ali al-Bayanouni, was even willing to concede, in a 2005 interview, that Nusayri-'Alawites are Muslim if they insist that that is who they are. See Mahan Abdein, "The Battle within Syria: An interview with Muslim Brotherhood Leader Ali Bayanouni," *Terrorism Monitor*, Vol. 3, Issue 16 (August 2005), available at http://www.james town.org/single/?no_cacheeq1&tx_ttnews%5Bswords %5D = 8fd5893941d69d0be3f378576261ae3e&tx_t tnews%5Bany_of_the_words%5D = Bayanouni&tx_tt news%5Btt_news%5D = 551&tx_ttnews%5Bback Pid%5D = 7&cHash = 65ac8ac6ec. In another interview with Aljazeera TV, al-Bayanouni asserted that Nusayri-'Alawites will not be threatened by regime change in Syria, as they are part of the cultural mosaic of the country, and have had their fair share of oppression by the

Asads. See Aljazeera Transcript, "Al-ikhwan al-Muslim-oon wel islah al-siyasi bi souriya," August 21, 2005, available at http://www.aljazeera.net/Channel/archive/archive?ArchiveId = 133546.

37. For a reliable discussion and overview of the "Shi'a Crescent" controversy, see Moshe Ma'oz, "The 'Shi'i Crescent': Myth and Reality," The Saban Center for Middle East Policy, The Brookings Institution, No. 15 (November 2007), pp. 1–33. Also, Michael Bröning, "Don't Fear the Shiites: The Idea of a Tehran Controlled Shiite Crescent over the Greater Middle East Is at Odds with Reality," *Internationale Politik und Gesellschaft*, No. 3 (2008), pp. 60–75.

38. Abdel-Stayyir Aal-Hussein, *Tahdheer al-berriyeh min nashat al-shi'a fi souriya* (2004), available at http://www.tawhed.ws/dl?i = 8in7fimb.

39. There is a large body of jihadist tracts that attack Hezbollah as a Zionist façade, simultaneously meant toc actually protect Israel and to polish the image of Shi'as as anything other than acolytes of the Zionists. Examination of this material is beyond the scope of this paper.

40. For a detailed analysis of this study, see Khalid Sindawi, "The Shiite Turn in Syria," *Current Trends in Islamist Ideology*, Vol. 8 (2009), pp. 82–107.

41. Al-Ma'ahad al-Duweli lil Dirasat al-Souriya, *Al-ba'ath al-shi'i fi souriya* [1919–2007] (2008), available at http://www.syrianstudies.org/Files/Microsoft%20Word%20-%20IISS_Shiasim_Research_V5.pdf.

42. Al-Suri's real name is Mustafa Abd al-Qadir Setmarian Nasar. He was a native of Aleppo (b. October 1958) who had been involved in the underground jihadist movement against the Syrian regime in the 1970s and spent fifteen years in various European countries, during the course of which he became a citizen of Spain. Al-Suri was involved in the Afghan and Algerian jihad, and was arrested in Quetta on October 31, 2005, by Pakistani authorities. For full biographical details, see Brynjar Lia, *Architect of Global Jihad; The Life of Al-Qaida Strategist Abu Mus'ab al-Sur* (New York: Columbia University Press, 2008). Al-Suri's most influential work was a 1,600-page volume published in January 2005 under the title *Da'wat al-muqawameh al-islamiyyah al-alamiyyah* ("The Global Islamic Resistance Call"), available at www.tawhed.ws/dl?i = f3r0098v. Translated portions are available in Lia, *Architect of Global Jihad*, p. 347–484.

43. Abu Mus'ab al-Suri (under the pen name Omar Abdul-Hakim), *Ahlul sunna fil sham fi muwajehet alnusayriyyeh wel salibiyyeh wel yahud,* Markaz alghuraba lil dirasat al-islamiyyeh (Afghanistan: June 22, 2000), available at http://www.tawhed.ws/r?i = jf3hqhhd. The essay runs to 69 pages. Al-Suri alludes to Shiite proselytizing by Iranians in Syria (p. 9), and promises that he will author a study on the topic later; he didn't seem to complete this goal. Lia, pp. 274–275.

44. Al-Suri, *Ahlul sunna fil sham,* p. 7.

45. Shortly after Asad's death, a hostile letter signed by "The Committee of Exiled Syrian Clerics" and primarily addressed to Bashar al-Asad and the Nusayri-'Alawite community set a high ceiling of terms by which the sect can be accepted by Muslims, primarily full repentance of all the tenets of Nusayri-'Alawism. See 'Bayan illa al-ta'ifa al-nusayriyyah,' available at http://www.tawhed.ws/r?i = kv6wr6by.

46. Al-Suri, *Ahlul sunna fil sham,* pp. 9–10. On the quietism of urban Damascenes, see Batatu, "Syria's Muslim Brethren," p. 18.

47. Al-Suri, *Ahlul sunna fil sham,* p. 27.

48. Al-Suri, *Ahlul sunna fil sham,* p. 49.

49. Al-Suri, *Ahlul sunna fil sham,* p. 51.

50. Al-Suri, *Ahlul sunna fil sham,* pp. 26–27. "Abu 'Aisheh al-Lubnani" is one of the jihadist leaders to whom this essay is dedicated.

51. Al-Suri, *Ahlul sunna fil sham,* p. 55.

52. Al-Suri, *Ahlul sunna fil sham,* p. 59–60.

53. Al-Suri, *Ahlul sunna fil sham,* pp. 62–63. In another essay under his name, al-Suri argues that the Syrian Muslim Brethren failed to mobilize other Muslim Brethren groups around the Middle East even though they were eager to join the jihad in Syria (p. 21) and that the jihadists were self-limiting by relying predominately on urban cadres without making use of the Bedouins or the Kurds (pp. 9–10). See Abu Mus'ab al-Suri, *Mulahadhat hawl al-tejrubah al-jihaddiyah fi sooriya,* undated,

available at http://www.tawhed.ws/r?i = 5vyty2zp. This essay seems to be a summary or adaptation of one of al-Suri's earliest works, a 900-page book in two volumes, published in Peshawar in May 1992 under the title *Al-thawrah al-islamiyyah al-jihadiyyah fi suria*. It is discussed at length in Lia, *Architect of Global Jihad*, pp. 58–65.

54. Abu Basseer al-Tartousi (real name: Abdul Mun'im Mustafa Halima), *Takkafal allahu li bil sham* ("Allah had entrusted me with Greater Syria") (March 2005), available at http://www.tawhed.ws/r?i = jr5s5rx6.

55. A compilation of such writings is available in most Islamic libraries and book shops. One example is Abi Abdul Rahman 'Adel bin Sa'ad, *Fadha'il al-sham* (Beirut: 2001). There is also a book attributed to Ibn Taymiyyah under the title of *Manaqib al-sham wa ahluhu* which I have not been able to find but which is cited often by jihadist writers.

56. Abu Basseer al-Tartousi, *Al-nidham al-soori wel wataniyyah* ("The Syrian Regime and Patriotism"), (January 2006), available at http://www.tawhed.ws/r?i = wzfd 74uh.

57. Martin Kramer, "Syria's Alawis and Shi'ism," *Shi-'ism, Resistance, and Revolution,* ed. Martin Kramer (Boulder, Colorado: Westview Press, 1987), pp. 237–54, available at http://www.geocities.com/martinkramerorg/Alawis.htm.

58. Nibras Kazimi, "Zarqawi's Anti-Shi'a Legacy: Original or Borrowed?" *Current Trends in Islamist Ideology*, Vol. 4 (2006), pp. 53–72.

59. Nibras Kazimi, "New Syrian Jihadist Group Delivers Anti-Alawite Calling Card," *Talisman Gate blog* (posted May 28, 2007) available at http://talismangate .blogspot.com/2007/05/new-syrian-jihadist-group-de livers-an ti.html.

60. This could be a play on words, *kalb* being the Arabic word for dog, and the name of the tribe that the Asads belong to, the al-Kalbiyyah.

61. Abu Jandal alleges that the assassination attempt was to coincide with Bashar's opening of the new soccer stadium of Aleppo, which occurred on April 3, 2007.

62. For a brief account of Jund al-Sham, see Stephen Ulph, "New Jihadist Group Emerges in Syria," *Terrorism Focus*, Vol. 2, Issue 12 (June 2005), available at http:// www.jamestown.org/single/?no_cache = 1&tx_ttnews%5 Bswords%5D = 8fd5893941d69d0be3f378576261ae3 e&tx_ttnews%5Bany_of_the_words%5D = Jund%20al -Sham&tx_ttnews%5Bpointer%5D = 3&tx_ttnews%5 Btt_news%5D = 512&tx_ttnews%5BbackPid%5D = 7& cHash = 2070bc537b.

63. The leader of the Islamic State of Iraq announced that al-'Absi was still alive in a speech he gave on February 14, 2008. The speech was an indication of the interest the jihadists in Iraq had taken in Greater Syria. See Nibras Kazimi, "Back to al-Baghdadi's Speeches," *Talisman*

Gate blog (posted April 18, 2008) and available at http://talismangate.blogspot.com/2008/04/back-to-al-baghdadis-speeches.html.

64. The plot was rather amateurish if judged by the sophistication of jihadist security tradecraft in Iraq. It was an in-house Fath al-'Islam plot, and does not seem to have involved either Abu Jandal's group or any outside help from other groups of jihadists. The suicide bomber was alleged to be a Saudi national. The details of the plot were revealed on official Syrian TV on November 5, 2008. Most of what was featured is available in transcript form from SANA at http://www.sana.sy/ara/2/2008/11/06/200295.htm (accessed November 6, 2008).

65. Sunni-Nusayri-'Alawite tensions in northern Lebanon are rooted in the events of the Lebanese Civil War. There is no indication that Salafists in Tripoli had instigated the latest round of clashes between the two sects. For a general overview concerning Sunni and Nusayri-'Alawite relations in 'Akkar, see Nibras Kazimi, "'Alawites and Sunnis Clash in Northern Lebanon," *Talisman Gate blog* (posted May 12, 2008), available at http://talismangate.blogspot.com/2008/05/sunnis-and-Alawites-clash-in-northern.html. Clashes have been ongoing as recently as August 2009. See Patrick Galey, "Sectarian rivalry simmers beneath calm Tripoli," *Daily Star* (August 25, 2009).

66. Abul Fadhl Madhi, *Sooriya: Alqa'ida al-sulbeh fir scenario al-taghyeer* ("Syria: The Firm Foundation in the

Scenario of Change"), (July 21, 2009), available at http://
alflojaweb.com/vb/showthread.php?t = 74628. Madhi's
essay was first discussed by Murad Batal al-Shishani, "Ji-
hadis Turn Their Eyes To Syria as Post-Iraq Theater of
Operations," *Terrorism Monitor*, Vol. 7 Issue 26, James-
town Foundation, available at http://www.jamestown
.org/programs/gta/single/?tx_ttnews%5Btt_news%5D
= 35435&cHash = 74e0a523e4.

67. Madhi alludes to a gentlemen's agreement by
which the jihadist refrained from striking against the
Syrian regime in return for safe passage to Iraq. This
agreement was ruptured by the Syrian state in a clampdown that included many other facets of Islamic revival,
including those loyal to the regime, in autumn 2005. Another jihadist source, a Saudi national named Faisal
Akbar, sets December 2005 as the date during which Syrian security forces initiated a round-up of jihadist elements. Although this source is controversial—it is
alleged that he admitted to jihadist responsibility in assassinating Hariri while giving testimony while under in-
carceration by Lebanese authorities, and later recanted
parts of this testimony—his testimony is valuable due to
the details provided of how jihadists operated on Syrian
territory. See Nibras Kazimi, "Analysis of the Faisal
Akbar testimony and how it relates to the Hariri assassination," *Talisman Gate blog* (posted November 5, 2007)
and available at http://talismangate.blogspot.com/2007/
11/analysis-of-faisal-akbar-testimony-and.html.

68. A pioneering study on sectarian discourse is available as a master's thesis by Torstein Schiotz Worren, presented at the Department of Sociology and Human Geography, University of Oslo (February 2007) under the title, *Fear and Resistance; The Construction of Alawi Identity in Syria.* It is available at http://www.duo.uio.no/publ/iss/2007/53268/fear_and_resistance.pdf. I have made use of the methodology used by Worren, essentially to categorize opinions drawn from a "closed" society, to write this section of the paper.

69. The author tried to enter Syria on a valid visa during August 2008, but was told at the border that his name appears on a list barring him from entry on grounds of security.

70. Yaron Friedman, "Al-Husayn ibn Hamdan al-Khasibi—A Historical Biography of the Founder of the Nusayri-'Alawite Sect," *Studia Islamica*, Vol. 93 (2001). Friedman argues that while the eponymous founder is taken to be Muhammed Ibn Nusair al-Namiri, the real founder and organizer of a distinct sect that drew inspiration from Ibn Nusayr was al-Khasibi.

71. Visit to Bab Al-Saghir cemetery, Damascus, March 5, 2006. The other companions allegedly entombed near Mu'awiya are Fadhaleh bin Obaid Allah, Suheil bin Handhalah, Aws al-Thaqafi, and Wa'ilah bin al-Asta'.

72. Visit to Bab al-Saghir cemetery, Damascus, June 30, 2007.

73. Visit to Sheikh Yabruq shrine, Aleppo, June 29, 2006. The date when the barracks was established is alternately attributed to either the time of the Egyptian Ibrahim Pasha's occupation of Syria or the time of the Ottomans. It seems to have been a cemetery before being converted into a barracks. According to Sunni sources, the shrine is attributed to Shamsuddine Muhammad bin Ahmed al-Rifa'i al-Ahmadi, in the Shumeissatiyyeh neighborhood, Abdul-Fattah al-Qal'aji, *Halab Al-Qadimah wa Al-Jadeedeh*, Al-Risala (Beirut: 1989), p. 223. This would explain the Rifa'i lodge built by Ottoman *vali* Muhammad Wahid right adjacent to the shrine. Many Nusayri-'Alawite published sources identify "Sheikh Yabruq" with al-Khasibi, alleging that it was a necessary ruse to mask the real identity of the person entombed there from Sunni retaliation.

74. A small community of Nusayri-'Alawites had survived in 'Anah until the 1970s at least, and anecdotally it is said that they still exist in the high hundreds, though it is unknown whether they still have religious cohesion. Another community survived, with religious leadership, in Baghdad and maintained contact with Levantine Nusayri-'Alawites until at least the middle of the nineteenth century. See Lyde, *The Asian Mystery*, p. 51.

75. Conversation, Damascus, June 22, 2006. The mosque was visited by the author on May 9, 2007.

76. Conversation, Qurrah al-Asad, March 16, 2006.

77. Conversation, Damascus, May 2, 2007.

78. Conversation, Abu Qobais valley, July 4, 2007.

79. Conversation, Nabi Younis shrine, May 10, 2007.

80. Conversation, Damascus, June 29, 2007.

81. Conversation with a Defense Ministry civilian employee, Wadi al-Ayoon, May 6, 2007. Even opponents of the regime acknowledge that Nusayri-'Alawites as a whole, especially in the mountains, have not seen their economic conditions improve drastically as a result of Asad rule. See Hanna Batatu, *Syria's Peasantry, the Descendants of Its Lesser Rural Notables, and Their Politics* (Princeton: Princeton University Press, 1999), p. 229. Other Nusayri-Alawites point out the number of their intellectuals who are active in leftist, Communist, or nationalist (specifically the Syrian Social Nationalist Party) opposition groups as evidence of widespread grievances among Nusayri-'Alawites against the regime. "My family is a third Communist, a third Ba'athist, and a third Syrian Social Nationalist," asserts a young Nusayri-'Alawite musician originally from the town of Dreikeesh (conversation, Tartous, May 8, 2007). "[The town of] Safita is all Syrian Social Nationalist; Bisnada is all Communist. 'Arif Dalilah, the dissident jailed by Bashar, is an 'Alawite." However, a large component of such enduring ideological party loyalties may be family affairs, inherited from the 1950s and 1960s when all these secular political currents were popular in the Nusayri-'Alawite mountains, and before the Ba'ath Party's leadership was settled in favor of a Nusayri-'Alawite clique led by officers Salah Jadid and Hafez al-Asad in the late 1960s, rather than expressions of opposition to the regime.

82. Conversation, Aleppo, March 9, 2006. Nusayri-'Alawite families would traditionally indenture their young daughters in the service of wealthy families in Syrian cities. One estimate has it that even by 1950, there were 10,000 such girls working as "domestic drudges in Damascus" alone. See Patrick Seale, *Asad: The Struggle for the Middle East* (Berkeley: University of California Press, 1988 [1989]), p. 23.

83. Conversation, Latakia, March 10, 2006. Nusayri-'Alawites view Syrian Christians (whose various denominations may constitute up to 10 percent of the country) as allies in the power balance versus Sunnis. See Worren, *Fear and Resistance*, pp. 77–78.

84. Conversation, Damascus, April 30, 2007.

85. Conversation, Aleppo, June 25, 2006. Al-Suri also alludes to this secret plan to absorb Homs into a separatist Nusayri-'Alawite state. See Al-Suri, *Ahlul sunna fil sham*, p. 12. There are dozens of villages and hamlets to the east and southeast of Homs that are Shi'a, an extension of the Shi'a presence in the Northern Beka'a valley of Lebanon. Some villages in the immediate vicinity of Homs have a history of *batini* activity, such as Qazhel. Furthermore, there was Shi'a migration to lands made cultivatable in the last two centuries east of Homs, even though it is asserted that some hamlets in this area had a continuing Shi'a presence since the eleventh century.

86. Conversation, Aleppo, May 12, 2007.

87. Conversation, provincial town, May 12, 2007.

88. Conversation, Damascus, June 20, 2006.

89. Conversation, Aleppo, March 9, 2006.

90. Conversation, Latakia, May 8, 2007.

91. Conversation, provincial town, May 5, 2007.

92. Conversation, Aleppo, March 9, 2006.

93. Conversation, Damascus, March 12, 2006.

94. Conversation, Zabadani, May 3, 2007.

95. Conversation, July 3, 2007.

96. Conversation, June 29, 2007.

97. Similarly, an adept of the Denderawiya Sufi order, who is hostile to Wahhabism, claimed (conversation, Damascus, March 6, 2006) that "the government now applies pressure on the Salafists. They are only active in outlying villages."

98. Conversation, Zarzoor, May 11, 2007.

99. Conversation, Nubbul, July 7, 2007. Nubbul has a registered population of approximately 23,000. The nearby town of Zahra's (formerly Naghawileh or Magha-wileh, and also Shi'a) has a registered population of 15,000. The other major Shi'a presence in northern Syria is the town of Al-Fou'a, near Idlib, with an estimated population of 9,000.

100. I met several young Syrians who claimed to have fought in Iraq in 2003 as part of a proto-jihadist mission encouraged and abetted by Syrian and Iraqi authorities at the time. A refugee from the Golan (conversation, March 2, 2006) asserted that he went to Iraq ahead of the war and was trained to fire an RPG-7 rocket by the Iraqi Republican Guard. He was later captured by the Americans and held for seven months. Upon his return

to Syria, he was arrested, and allegedly tortured, by Syrian security for six weeks. They accused him of being a spy for the Americans. He broke out in expletives directed at the security building where he was held as we passed it in his taxi. The young sheikh of the historic al-Dakkak Mosque in the Maydan quarter of Damascus (conversation, March 5, 2006) casually said, "I fought in Iraq under the guidance of Dr. Bashar al-Asad."

About the Author

NIBRAS KAZIMI is a visiting scholar at the Hudson Institute. Previously, he directed the Research Bureau of the Iraqi National Congress in Washington, D.C., and Baghdad and was a pro bono adviser to the Higher National Commission for De-Ba'athification, which he helped establish and staff. He also contributed regular columns to the *New York Sun* and *Prospect Magazine* (UK).

Kazimi's research focuses on the growing threat of jihadism in the Middle East, as well as prospects for democracy in the region. His primary interest is the national security of Iraq and how threats to the nascent democracy there are enabled and coordinated by regional Middle Eastern actors and factors. He travels widely; recently he visited Turkey, Iraq, Iran, Lebanon, Syria, Egypt, and Jordan.

Herbert and Jane Dwight
Working Group on
Islamism and the
International Order

HOOVER INSTITUTION
STANFORD UNIVERSITY

The Herbert and Jane Dwight Working Group on Islamism and the International Order seeks to engage in the task of reversing Islamic radicalism through reforming and strengthening the legitimate role of the state across the entire Muslim world. Efforts will draw on the intellectual resources of an array of scholars and practitioners from within the United States and abroad, to foster the pursuit of modernity, human flourishing, and the rule of law and reason in Islamic lands—developments that are critical to the very order of the international system.

The Working Group is chaired by Hoover fellows Fouad Ajami and Charles Hill with an active participation of Director John Raisian. Current core membership includes Russell A. Berman, Abbas Milani, and Shelby Steele, with contributions from Zeyno Baran, Reul Marc Gerecht, Ziad Haider, R. John Hughes, Nibras Kazimi, Habib Malik, and Joshua Teitelbaum.

INDEX